A Stoma Named Stanley

Reflections From A Brief Nursing Career

JD Moore

Copyright © 2021 J D Moore
All rights reserved

Disclaimer: all names of people are fictional for the purposes of privacy. Any similarity to real persons, living or dead, is not intended by the author. Memories are imperfect, the contents are to the best of the author's knowledge.

No part of this book may be reproduced, or stored in a retrieval system, or transmitted in any form or by any means, electronic, mechanical, photocopying, recording, or otherwise, without express written permission of the publisher.

ISBN-13: 978-0-578-34004-3

Cover design by: Delany

To Meme.

Table Of Contents

Preface	9
First Year	11
Visual Observations	16
Tree Felling Hard	22
Maggot Mania	27
Oxygen	32
Suicide	37
Nursing For The Few	44
Scabies	46
"Stanley" The Stoma	51
Frequent Fliers, Drug Alley, Full Moon	53
Serious Errors	57
Nursing Informatics	59
Gastro	62
Comfort	64
Wood-Chipper Threesome/Mangled à Trois	66
Skin Is An Organ	70
Death And Fluid	73

Paediatrics In Emergency	76
End-Stage Cancer	78
Amputations Galore	80
Snake Bite	82
Convict	84
Endotracheal Intubating	87
Motorcycle	90
Guilt	92
Inter-Hospital Transfer	94
Spousal Confusion	99
Encephalopathy	101
Lockdown Area for Violent Patients	
#1	103
#2	105
Bus Driver Stroke	107
Cannot See	109
Charlie	111
Too Much Power	116
Living Remote	119
Death at 36,000 Feet	122
Reflections On Nursing	126

Afterword	**132**
About the Author	**140**

Preface

Early on before any nursing career ideas formulated, I read a book called "Trauma Junkie", by Janice Hudson, about a flight nurse in San Jose, California. I found her experience fascinating with stories of incredible rescues. I devoured books relating to trauma, rescue, mountain climbing, and rock climbing.

As a fixed-wing private pilot, I initially considered flying rescue missions as a career. However, these rescues are largely done by helicopters and piloted by ex-military pilots. I was neither.

In discussing our future, my partner and I decided nursing would be a good 'retirement' degree to obtain with only a couple of years of education and would get me on my way to working in a hospital. As we researched nursing schools, we noticed the nursing major was saturated (very few openings) in the U.S., and most programs were very competitive.

Staying local, I began a pre-nursing program towards a bachelor's degree in San Francisco. However, this was no guarantee of admission to a U.S. nursing program. My partner and I agreed that moving country would be beneficial to both of us: nursing schools were wide open for students; gaining citizenship in my partner's home country was fairly uncomplicated; he'd be returning to his roots.

After a year of pre-nursing education, we moved from my native country. I felt a bit displaced; my comfort zone, familiar surroundings, a cushion of friends and family were not present. My spouse was still in the states finalising household and financial matters. I was faced with a new career, surroundings, cultures, and customs. I wanted very much to assimilate, to belong to this new community. And regardless of some animosity towards me as a foreigner, I eventually made several very good friends. Their acceptance and warmth towards me made all the difference.

My foundation courses from the San Francisco university were transferrable to my new country's university nursing program. I was on my way. After two years of study, I had a bachelor's degree and was a registered nurse.

As pilots, we refer to getting our license as our "ticket". Effectively, entry into a pilot society, where we fly airplanes on a whim that take us places, see and do new things. Similarly, with nursing, I had effectively secured an entry ticket, a pass, into a world that few people experience. It was a rare opportunity and I was ecstatic.

What followed, upon completing my nursing degree and gaining employment, was a truly humbling and horrendous experience.

First Year

After graduating from nursing school, I applied for and was offered a very limited and coveted position in the Graduate Nurse Program at a local hospital. The job, one year in length with two differing ward placements, is a paid position that few nurse graduates are awarded and as such is a real privilege. Assigned to a clinical nursing coach and educator, it is designed to support newly registered nurses (RNs), providing them opportunities to reinforce their clinical and theoretical skills in a hospital setting.

During the first placement, I would spend about five months working in the surgical ward at a regional hospital. The ward was for pre-operative and post-operative patients; that is, preparing patients for surgery and then caring for them post-surgery. This was a heavy ward, flat-out, full-throttle all the time. The broad range of medical conditions that required surgical intervention was many.

The surgeries we prepped daily, included: appendectomy; partial colectomy; cholecystectomy; coronary artery bypass; debridement of wound, burn, or infection; hemorrhoidectomy; hysterectomy; inguinal hernia repairs; mastectomy; tonsillectomy;

prostatectomy. Post-operative care included the above and the occasional stab wounds, gunshot wounds, shampoo bottles removed from the rectum, dog bite wounds, and broken bones.

I was certainly challenged daily as a new RN. My workload was nearly doubled as I was carrying a full patient load and learning how to be a nurse, including: gaining proficiency in medical conditions requiring surgical procedures; acquiring and retaining knowledge and an understanding of all surgery basics on my patients; managing and mastering the particular care required pre- and post-surgical procedure; learning about new medications, the pharmacology (drug classification, side/adverse effects, and dosage), and how to pronounce the drugs properly. Regardless of the demanding road ahead and despite what unfolded over the next five months, I maintained a positive attitude and outlook.

After only a couple of weeks into my new position, the nurse educator and coach on this ward shadowed me during my shifts. "Ms. As" claimed I was falling behind the other graduate nurses. I was grateful to receive her help and extensive knowledge, to have her teach me how to improve my practice. The grad year is a learning opportunity to help new grads get through medication errors and mishaps, of all kinds, in the safety of the coach and other RNs on the ward. But each shift would bring new problems.

Ms. As would scold me in front of my colleagues, pull me aside into an empty room, or take me into her office. Her feedback was constant criticism, never giving me a positive word of encouragement. I asked her to please offer me some antidote, some positive words to keep my spirits up. She refused.

"Why can't you pronounce all our drug names properly? You seem to struggle with some names such a Benazepril, Moexipril, Ustekinumab, and Levetiracetam. We are running out of resources for helping you. This is your last opportunity." Ms. As went on to suggest I do not repeat mistakes, including: using jargon; poor handwriting, and a messy shift planner; do not ask for help with my patient load of six; do ask for help with my patient load; stop asking the wrong questions at handover.

"Do you have a learning disability or mental health issues?" The coach began asking me questions like this in another impromptu meeting at the end of my shift. Sure I was tired, but did I hear her correctly? "We offer mental health services through a hotline, do you have that number?"

Bullying is commonplace in nursing, it is appalling and creates a very toxic culture. I was bullied relentlessly by this nursing coach. She was merciless and vindictive, often holding me two or three hours past my shift (without pay) to berate me. She created a climate of intimidation and humiliation, including threats of dismissal and loss of my nursing license.

Other nurses on the ward began to notice the discrepancy, the discrimination this coach had towards me; they offered to help. The hospital's head of nursing education was called in to review my work during a morning shift. She spent several hours observing and documenting my nursing practice and upon completion would present her findings to the hospital's nursing board. The nurses that supported me were there during the testing to provide positive feedback to the educator. She found my work exemplary and requested this particular coach abandon her prejudicial agenda.

Finally, after months of trying and failing to sort out a middle-ground with this coach and hospital management, I called on the nurses' union for advice and obtained legal counsel. The union was very helpful and supportive in consulting me both personally and in my legal quest. A union lawyer called me and advised that he be present as my representative for future meetings with hospital management, including the coach. This simple gesture was overwhelming; I was in tears.

Things improved quickly after several meetings and I was free of this situation. The coach came up to me shortly after the last meeting with my legal counsel and hugged me, crying, stating, "You have improved so much. I'm so proud of you." My career moved on and advanced rapidly but for years after this experience, I still was reeling, still utterly and completely baffled at what had happened and why.

Throughout my nursing career, I worked as a registered nurse on the surgical ward, neurology & stroke ward (most challenging), emergency department (most rewarding), and as a clinical, senior nurse for discharge planning. This book provides stories from my experiences.

Visual Observations

A 78-year-old woman arrived on our neurology ward at 10 PM with a primary diagnosis of a urinary tract infection (UTI) and some associated delirium. We'll call her Ms. Sue (not her real name). She was placed in the only available bed on the ward in our cognition assessment unit, a sub-ward reserved for severe cognitive decline, with eight total patients amongst four rooms. Ms. Sue, although complaining of being tired, was alert and chatty.

I did not notice anything unusual about her. The plan was to keep her overnight for safety and observations, discharging her the following day to see her general practitioner for follow-up. This is common practice for delirium patients.

Her daughter accompanied her to the room and we all spoke briefly, while dressing her in a hospital gown, about Ms. Sue's symptoms and any important details about her medical history. The patient adjacent to Ms. Sue's bed, behind a drawn curtain, was fast asleep. I did some admission observations/vital signs, recorded medical and other required information and doctors' orders were as follows: for bed rest; monitoring her toilet frequency; pain management; and re-evaluation during the next morning's rounds.

The Cognitive Assessment Unit is a lockdown unit reserved for patients with cognitive impairments, this might include: severe dementia; aggravated behaviours from cognitive impairment; and functional impairment from a cerebral or brain hypoxia (brain injury) incident.

In the unit, during night shifts, the rules for these types of patients include: allow plenty of rest; provide low stimulus; visual (non-tactile) observations only unless the patient has specific orders or requires intervention during the night (eg. disruptive, unusual behaviour including yelling-out, climbing out of bed, deteriorating health). There are two RNs and occasionally access to a nurse assistant for extra help. Nurses share the "rounding" observation frequencies (every 2 hours), including a standard five "P"s: potty, pain, position, possessions, and peaceful environment.

Nighttime rounding checks are a quiet walk through the room, often around the sides or foot of the beds, listening for breathing sounds, including chest movement to record a respiratory rate, and check if they are awake and if they need anything. The nurse-patient ratio is higher in this unit due to the risks involved with these types of patients. They can become violent at any time without warning. We wear pagers/alarms on our belts with a pull-string and button for emergency calls to security.

During this particular night, most of the patients slept quietly. There were a couple of patients calling out and usually they need help to the toilet and then settle back down, falling asleep. As I performed my first set of rounding checks in Ms. Sue's room at midnight, she was snoring quite loudly and appeared to be sleeping well. A check of her respiratory rate showed she was within normal limits and I moved on to the next patient. During the second set of checks at approximately 0200 hours there was something odd about Ms. Sue. This is a nurse's intuition and it is something we absolutely cannot ignore in our profession.

I once discussed this intuition with a fellow senior nurse and she said, "If you ever have any question in your mind that something isn't right or doesn't feel right about a patient, you have to do something, some intervention." This reminded me of a patient who kept complaining about a stomach ache after lunch. No one thought much of it, perhaps just indigestion. I escalated the man's concerns as he did not appear well at all and it turned out he had an abdominal bleed.

I decided to do a full set of observations, vital sign checks, on Ms. Sue and I wasn't too worried about waking her up as she was not a typical cognitive unit patient. She was a 'simple' UTI admission and would likely be discharged post an intravenous antibiotic course. Further, she was not dangerous nor did she have dementia; she had mild delirium. What happened next would change my perspective on my nursing practice, particularly concerning rounding.

Ms. Sue stopped responding shortly after I placed a blood pressure cuff on her upper arm and tightened it. She had no response to a gentle poke in the ear with a tympanic (ear) thermometer. So I called out her name. Then I squeezed her on the trapezius muscle in the shoulder, there was nothing. I called the team leader and explained the situation; we then called the on-call nighttime intern doctor.

This doctor does hospital rounds as needed, assessing patients, prescribing medications, and performing procedures. We relayed to him the problem and scenario. We had an unresponsive patient and these were her vital signs, to which the doctor replied they were busy and would be up as soon as possible. I did a couple more checks for patient responsiveness, including a 'sternal rub'. I did this hard against her chest. She did not budge, no response, but she continued snoring loudly. The situation was strange. I called the doctor again.

Two doctors arrived at approximately 0300 hours. They did some of the same checks I had done and realised this patient was in bad shape. They presumed a stroke and we rushed her down for a CT scan of her brain. The CT technician, doctors, and I were all in the observation room looking down at the computer monitor showing her brain scan. She had a very large darkened area covering most of her brain to which we all agreed was from a massive bleed.

The tragedy here was not the moment we ascertained imminent death or a terminal illness but it was knowing the impact on the families and friends. As hospital staff mentally process such findings, we do not dwell on catastrophic outcomes, we get on with our jobs. That does not mean we are uncompassionate. We are here to treat many patients in the hospital and this requires us to be compassionate but also remain detached. Upon returning to the ward with Ms. Sue, we moved her to a private room that was now available.

I called her family and advised them to please come to the hospital as soon as possible, Ms. Sue had only a couple of hours to live. This shocked the family considering she was admitted with a UTI and some minor confusion.

Even after several years of nursing, there are still some surprising cases and this was one of them. Neither did the doctors nor nurses on shift that night predict this outcome. As a result, I became more conscientious at checking patients' cognition vital signs during night shift rounds. In other words, snoring is not necessarily indicative of a healthy patient.

Ms. Sue died about 30 minutes after the family arrived. The only good part of this story is the family was able to be with her before and at her time of death. I was grateful to facilitate her family in these last few moments. There was no chance Ms. Sue could register her loved ones were around her, but perhaps she felt them near spiritually or metaphysically.

Tree Felling Hard

Room five on this neurology ward is usually reserved for single patients that require a more solitary experience or perhaps more peaceful surroundings. As you enter, there is a short passageway; beyond the wall to the right is an ensuite that occupies a third of the room. Standing at the door looking down this passageway, you see the head of the bed against the left wall and part of a window looking out to a parking area. We have this room 'reserved' because it can accommodate a small family gathering without the prying eyes of other patients and families. This room can be used for the very sick: traumatic head injuries; incapacitated or immobile; dying or palliative; or physically fine but emotionally crying out and disruptive to other patients.

Doing my rounds this morning, as discharge planner, I went to a patient in room five. Ms. Amara arrived the night prior, was in her early 60s, a bit heavy-set, a gracious woman. Knocking and upon entering, I introduced myself and could see she was in the bed moaning and wriggling in pain. She was waiting for her morning medications from the nurses starting at 0700 hours. Because she was in room five, she would have her meds by about 0800 hours due to the sequence of rooms. That is, the rooms prior to hers, one through four were multi-patient rooms. I reassured her by stating that I could provide her pain medications now. I knew from her chart and handover from the night staff why she was in hospital but I didn't know the history of her injuries.

I provided her mostly analgesic medications to which she was very thankful. Her breakfast was just being delivered and I helped set up the plate of food and adjust her bed for ease of access. I explained that once the medications took effect, I would return to help her shower with a nursing assistant. Discharge planners are not required to perform nursing support, but when the wards are understaffed, we help where we can.

Morning nursing rounds are the busiest time on the wards. Nurses are charged with administering morning medications. Typically the largest amount of medications given during the day is in the morning time, including: intravenous drips; antibiotics; morphine; and necessary co-nursing signatures for 'dangerous drugs'. In addition, there are showers, toileting, bed making, tidying up the room, and note-taking. If a patient is palliative, has had a stroke, and/or is completely reliant on staff for every physical need, obviously this takes a considerable amount of time, effort, and coordinating with other members of the team.

Returning to Ms. Amara's room, she was seated on the bed, had a cane in her right hand using it to swing her legs off the bed and shuffle down to her wheelchair. I was curious at that moment watching her, how long had she been like this, in a wheelchair, incapacitated? How experienced was she at getting out of bed and into her wheelchair? These are some of the questions we usually ask prior to mobilising patients; we try to offer them as much independence as possible.

I told her I assumed she was feeling the effects of the analgesia and was ready to get to the toilet and shower. I wanted her to be feeling no pain so we could more easily move her around, in and out of the shower. She agreed and was already attempting to get to the toilet without ringing the nursing call bell. I suggested that while she's in the hospital it is wise to use the call bell for all mobilising so someone is at the ready just in case there's a misstep. She assured me she would use the call bell but I wasn't convinced considering her current predicament at the foot of the bed trying to get into the wheelchair alone. She reluctantly asked for my help.

Ms. Amara had come into hospital, she explained, because of her husband's heart condition (he was also admitted, staying on the ward one floor above) and her excruciating back pain. This wasn't new to her, she often came to the hospital after over-doing it at home. She had some lower-limb paralysis resulting in limited use of her legs. Various movements could trigger a back spasm just by sitting, standing, or moving. I asked her how she got this way?

"My husband was up in a tree", she relayed, shaking her head, looking down, her face grimaced, "with a chainsaw, on a ladder." Ms. Amara continued describing the horrifying details of what happened next.

"He was trying to trim a massive branch. He told me to hold the ladder so he would be stable and not fall. The next minute, I didn't see it, I heard it, half the tree fell to the ground and bounced. What I remember next was lying on my back, looking up at the sky, stunned. The branch had come down on top of me, breaking my back."

I could hardly believe what she was telling me. She further explained she was still married to him and he now has a serious heart condition. "I sometimes wish he were dead. This all happened about seven years ago." Because he was in the hospital for several days, her managing alone at home was getting difficult and she decided it was best to admit herself too.

Watching her struggle to move her body below her waist, I found myself casting blame on her husband. Was he irresponsible with his wife's life? He requested her protection for himself only to result in unthinkable harm. It was an accident, after all, but tree felling is serious business. Her story was a tale of how quickly one's life can change; a single life-altering event. A seemingly harmless day of tree trimming and spotting when suddenly there was a horrific accident; it caught two people totally by surprise.

What other overwhelmingly impressive accidents happen between caring couples? I've felt nervous when my partner passes cars in heavy traffic. Are we meant to blindly trust the person with whom we've committed our love and lives? Would my partner and I have done the same as Ms. Amara and her husband? I reflected on how this could happen to us. I hoped, of course, we are more cautious.

Maggot Mania

There are many hospital stories about maggots living and crawling on people. These stories are commonplace for emergency department staff. A fly lays its eggs in a human's open wound and then the eggs hatch into a larval stage feeding on live and/or necrotic tissue. The problems begin when the maggots get out of control.

A woman in her 50s presented to emergency via ambulance due to falling down steps at a friend's house. The story she tells is something like this: house-sitting for a friend of a friend; didn't know the terrain very well; fell outside in the dark, it was midnight or so; was drunk "usually drinking a lot"; didn't realise there was a head wound; didn't realise there were maggots in the head wound. In emergency, the nurses counted 80 maggots crawling around her scalp wound and in her ears. She was cleaned up and sent to a ward. Within a couple of hours, she self-discharged and returned the following day with yet many more burrowing maggots.

The problem with her story is that the maggots take some time to develop in a wound; the wound has to be open for a good length of time for flies to be present and lay eggs. As such, we deduced the fall and head injury were several days prior to her presentation or a second, more recent, head injury that was worse than the initial impalement. Scanning through hospital records, the woman had no clinical mental illness history, but she had a serious drinking problem.

I went to her room for a discharge planning consultation. Entering the single room, it was bright with sunlight streaming in through two large windows. Ms. Sarah was laying on the bed (in Fowler's position or upright about 35-40 degrees) staring up at the ceiling until she saw me and turned her head to say hello. She was disheveled, her hair was a tangled mess, dirty fingernails, and wearing a grubby t-shirt even after being in hospital for 24 hours. From my brief chat with her nurse, Ms. Sarah was non-compliant with most things, including cleanliness.

We briefly exchanged friendly banter about nasty bugs followed by my asking her, cautiously, about her background and recent events in her life. Discharge planners often find they are consultants to patients and families about their future care. In part, like a social worker, we assess the personal and social needs of the patient and their families; we discuss community assistance resources to empower the patient and family; resources they may need to further their well-being and improve living situations. We gather details including: how the house is set-up for care, if at all; who are the carers, if any; what obstacles exist (no ramp into house, poorly arranged furniture, too much furniture); we consult patients and their families on their options for post-discharge.

I asked Ms. Sarah if I could have a look at her wound. She stated that the dressing on her head was always falling off and in an undignified fashion found herself sitting on it. She laughed at this confession, full of smiles and awkward quips. On the back of her head was a deep wound together with a repulsive rotting flesh odour. Ms. Sarah simplified the predicament, "I drink and I fall down". She was asked by a family friend to house sit for another friend. She usually lives with her mother and this was a good break from home life. She remembers when she fell outside, "It was dark and I must have hit my head on a cement step. I was out cold for about 20 hours on the ground when the neighbour, peeking through a hedge, found me." To the hospital staff, the timeframe seemed a bit unlikely.

Ms. Sarah was a character. I encouraged her to stay in the hospital and finish out her treatment. She said she would stay the course. We spoke about alcohol abuse and how and why she started drinking. I was not going to cast blame, rather, I wanted to let her talk, to let out frustrations and I would listen. The unequivocal question was, how did she get to the point of a maggot infestation in her head wound, and ears? Apparently, she had no psychological or mental health history or she did and it was in another county or state? It was truly baffling.

I have seen older patients with poor hygiene management, as a result of neglect, present to hospital with maggot infestations, or perineal (private parts) sores due to weeks of sitting in faecal matter. But I've not seen someone as young as Ms. Sarah unless they have a mental health disorder. I briefly consulted with the staff psychiatrist and she assured me that Ms. Sarah was not a risk to herself or others and that she had the mental capacity for self-care per several psychiatric exams (taken while in hospital). Patients that "pass" hospital exams showing capacity (for self-care) are left to their own devices and upon discharge may return to their home. If, however, she had some incapacity she would have been discharged to a long-term care facility such as for rehabilitation or even an aged care facility for a time.

It is a human right to be free from officialdom or interference from powers that be. Interfering or stepping in to take control of another's life is a particularly sensitive subject concerning the elderly, people with seemingly odd behaviours, and the homeless. We are fortunate in civilised societies that there are professionals with whom we can rely to protect our wellbeing. Leave well enough alone, someone once said.

After a couple of hours visiting with Ms. Sarah, I told her I would return the following day as we needed to arrange for a nurse visit to her home to check her sutures. We would arrange for a nurse to dress her head wound every few days until her next doctor's visit. She was so encouraged by this, she asked if we could be friends and go for coffee? I was a bit taken aback but not entirely surprised by her offer. I imagined, from her perspective, she felt a connection perhaps because I had taken the time to sit with her, let her talk, quietly listen, and offer compassionate feedback.

  Maggot stories occur all too often; these stories are usually found in scary police shows or horror movies. But nurses experience all of it; we see and make the best that all mankind throws at us.

Oxygen

Nurses are usually regarded as reputable citizens, people with integrity. This is how I considered myself. For example, we are sometimes asked to witness the signing of legal documents, statutory declarations. But occasionally, there are situations when a patient will question our character.

Many of my patients are sent home with a new oxygen requirement or prescription. The patient needs an ongoing oxygen supply at home for various reasons. As a discharge planner, I am responsible for organising the doctor's order.

A patient, the hospital was discharging shortly, required oxygen at home. There are several steps to complete an oxygen discharge, including: an eight-page government-subsidised funding application for the local oxygen supply company; calling the oxygen supply company to check if they have oxygen canisters/supplies; organising the delivery of the canisters/supplies timely; educating the patient to the risks and potential dangers of oxygen in the home; and organising a nursing company to provide a nurse visit the first few days.

The form, completed by an RN, requires a doctor's signature and medication details for the oxygen (a drug) and some basic medical information about the patient. The form took some time to complete due to the following: tracking down the doctor to complete his portion of the form and run a set of diagnostic tests; getting copies of medicare and identification cards from the patient; ensuring someone was home to receive the canisters; and contacting at least two family members, close friends, or legitimate contacts willing to be on the form as collateral.

On this particular day, I had four wards to manage as a discharge planner. Two were respiratory wards, one cardiac, and one general medical. I had a student with me for the day and we were doing ward rounds visiting with patients needing discharge planning consultations. My student was a young woman, new to the country. She was very soft-spoken, eager to learn, and asked many questions. Together we briefly scanned this new patient's chart for current residence, age, gender, hospital presentation, and government funding.

She stood a short distance behind me as we entered the room for "oxygen man." There were three doctors in the corridor, just outside, talking and typing on their mobile computers. The single room was cool, bordering on freezing, like most rooms; the sun was shining down on the bed and an empty chair sat in the corner. The male patient, we'll call him Mr. Steffan, was seated at the side of the bed, in his wheelchair in the sunshine. It was a beautiful day outside. A blanket covered the lower half of his body. Mr. Steffan smiled, rearranged his oxygen mask, greeting us as I explained our role in discharge planning. My student listened and took notes.

Mr. Steffan was in the respiratory ward for poor lung function. He wasn't an old man; he did not have dementia; he was, however, described in staff documentation as a bit gruff. He confided that he had been a smoker for most of his life. What he needed was home oxygen to facilitate his discharge tomorrow. Not surprisingly, many discharges are at the "drop of a hat" planning by the doctors and thus require all staff to scramble to facilitate a patent's timely departure.

I explained to him that getting this application started immediately would be crucial and would need to be expedited for his discharge; he was happy to comply. After a bit of digging to find the necessary identification cards in his overnight bags, he readily handed them to me and with my student, we went to the ward's copier machine at the end of the corridor. Upon arrival, there was a sign on the copier, "Under repair". So we went to another ward across the hall. Someone was using it and we waited our turn.

Once all our copying was complete, we went back to his room to return the cards. I asked Mr. Steffan where he wanted his cards returned, he motioned to his wallet sitting on top of a bag. I placed the cards in the wallet and left immediately to complete the application form.

Upon returning to Mr. Steffan's room with the form to get his signature, the blanket was gone from his lap and I was taken aback at what I discovered: he was a double amputee above the knees (AKA: above-knee amputation). When he saw me, his face was red with frustration. He was irate claiming I had stolen his identification cards. His voice was raised and he was telling me I was a horrible person to steal his important cards. "These cards are my lifeline!", he sputtered. I tried to calm him down and remind him I put the cards in his wallet after I returned them. But he continued accusing me of stealing the cards. I raised my voice over him, telling him that nurses don't steal.

"Nurses are upstanding, well-regarded, honest citizens in the community; we don't steal!" I felt the collective gaze of doctors in the hallway outside the room. My student was startled at the confrontation. I realised we were causing a bit of a scene and I took his hand, gently reassuring him, showing him his wallet. He looked inside to find the cards. He smiled a sigh of relief. Upon that revelation, I explained we finished the application and the oxygen would be delivered to his home the following day.

Later that evening, I reflected on the anger I had expressed and my lack of compassion for this man. I should have put myself in his situation: he was nervous, worried, concerned, and probably a bit frightened. I had no idea what he was going through in life, what complications he had endured up to this point. He wasn't being malicious and I needn't have raised my voice. However, it was unfair of him to falsely accuse me and I felt in that moment, I needed to disprove the false accusation and reassure him at the same time.

    Of course, nurses need to take all accusations from their patients seriously and follow up. We are under intense scrutiny in our practice and are required to provide the utmost professionalism and care to patients.

Suicide

I recall it was a gorgeous morning driving to the hospital. The sun was a bright glow just barely over the tops of the foothills; birds were flittering about, dew still on the ground of the many pastures along the route. My morning was very unlike Ms. Michelle's, her whole world came into razor-sharp focus in a matter of moments.

Mr. Darren, a 35-year-old male, tall, muscular, fit, was found by his wife, Michelle, hanging in the garage by a fine ligature. With the help of one of their two sons, she was able to cut him down and begin CPR. She estimated that she found him five or ten minutes post-hanging due to a comment by one of his sons; the son was just talking to Darren out in the garage when he left his dad alone.

Paramedics arrived and assessed his vital signs, breathing was shallow. Sadly, he was unresponsive to stimuli, his eyes staring straight ahead, pupils dilated and fixed, no longer reacting to the light. The lack of oxygen, even for mere minutes to the brain (hypoxia), had resulted in severe brain damage. Interestingly enough, the body does function in basic mode: laboured breathing, erratic temperature, and small seizures. He was not placed on life support as he was just able to maintain an airway, albeit difficult. After arriving at emergency and then being transferred to a single room in the ward, Mr. Darren was settled.

It was haunting, to me at least, the house on the corner block where the suicide boy had lived. It wasn't a pretty house with its overgrown weeds, bad front lawn, and weather-beaten shingles on the windows. I never noticed this house until I learned what happened inside.

One morning as my parents were driving us to school, they informed me and my sister that the teenager living there had committed suicide. I was immediately struck by curiosity and a sense of sadness. I didn't know him but remember seeing him a few times around the neighbourhood.

I was completely fascinated by his suicide. I wanted to know how he did it, what it meant, why someone does it, who does it, and what makes life so bad someone would choose to kill themselves? I imagined he hung himself. I kept my thoughts, emotions, and questions to myself. I was ten-years-old.

When I turned 18, I signed up as a volunteer at the local suicide prevention centre (crisis hotline). With training completed, I was left on my own to field calls from the public.

Late one afternoon, volunteer Rima was working alone when she took a call at about 5 PM. As volunteers, we record basic information about the caller: their name or pseudonym; was the call for them or someone they know; and details about the crisis are recorded as well. These help the volunteer who is on the next shift to get acquainted with all previous shift's calls. This is in case there is a repeat caller, we want to be acquainted with their crisis. I was on the next shift after Rima and when I arrived I could see she was distraught by a recent call. I suggested she get some debrief counseling from our staff psychiatrist.

We spoke about the call and went through her notes together. The caller stated his name was Roger and it was his real name. As he described to Rima his feelings of dread, emptiness, and thoughts of suicide, she could hear the pain and suffering in his voice. He sounded very flat and dejected. He told her the story of why he wanted to end his life; he felt he had killed his best friend in a 4-wheel driving accident. He was the driver and his friend was thrown from the truck and died at the scene. It was truly heartbreaking, as are most of these calls. He told Rima his method of suicide was a gunshot to his head. Since he had intent, she was obligated to get him help immediately.

Eventually, Rima convinced Roger to give her his address so she could send help. Rima didn't necessarily need him to tell her his phone number or address as we had old-school technology available through a police trace, a direct police line.

When Rima showed me his address, I was caught off-guard. This was the home address of one of my best friends. This was her husband calling! I panicked, wondering if Josephine was with him and in danger? I asked Rima if she confirmed if anyone was with him? Roger stated that he was alone.

Our goal as crisis hotline volunteers is to listen and provide immediate emergency telephone counseling. Often we talk the caller "down" from their heightened state and try to convince them not to kill themselves but instead seek professional counseling. We suggest a visit with a good friend, talk to someone they trust. For Roger, Rima was able to do this for him. He said he would call his wife and talk things through with her. Still, a "welfare check" officer was sent to his home.

My dilemma, and something I struggled with was, should I go against policy? It was ethically inappropriate for me to call and inform my best friend about her husband's call to our crisis line. This was confidential information to be kept between Roger, the crisis volunteers, and public service personnel such as police.

In the end, Roger shot himself in the head a couple of weeks later. I learned this through Josephine. She knew he had called our hotline and asked me if I knew about his call? I confirmed I knew about the situation, the call, but explained I could not ethically divulge his call or details, or betray his trust (regardless that it was policy).

This was a very difficult time for Josephine and I was as supportive as possible during the year that followed. She went down a hole, was medicated, and decided to stay with her parents for some time. There was a memorial held for Roger after his burial. I attended the gathering and wanted to talk to Roger's mother, Alice.

I met Alice sitting outside with a cup of tea in her hand, her eyes were tired, shallow, her face sullen. I knelt beside her at the edge of her chair and began with my condolences and how very sorry I was. She was polite and smiled. I told her of my relationship with Josephine and her eyes lit up and she looked right at me. I explained about a program we had at the volunteer centre for survivors of sudden death. I described further how welcoming and understanding the team was, that there would be other survivors. It would be a time to listen or talk or just be near others sharing similar grief. I gave Alice the location and time. Later, I heard she attended and was overwhelmed with a sense of relief and comfort - having met the team and other survivors.

As nurses walk the corridors towards their patient's rooms, we prepare ourselves as best we can prior to entering. I went to check on Mr. Darren and was told the family was with him.

It is a sinking feeling, in your heart, knowing something horrible, tragic, and surreal is about to reveal itself beyond the door. It is stepping into a cold, white, sterile room where the only life is the colourfully clothed, warm bodies surrounding a single bed. The moment I entered Mr. Darren's room, you could feel in the air just how much the wife and sons were beyond devastated. With their expressionless faces saying everything, I spoke first. I could not think of any words that would console this family except, "I'm so very sorry."

Talking to Ms. Michelle, she explained the background of what, perhaps, led to his suicide. She described his inability to communicate or express his pain from a childhood wrought with suffering, trauma, and fear. As a child he was raped by his mother's boyfriend. "He couldn't deal with the 'freak' he felt he was from the child abuse". Furthermore, along with his mother and younger sister, he was in a horrific car accident that killed his sister. Ms. Michelle explained he blamed himself for not saving her.

The family stepped out while we nurses gave him a bed bath and massage to his arms, hands, and feet. I cleaned his face noticing red ligature marks across his neck, changed his white hospital gown and pillowcase. Knowing the history behind his attempted suicide, as explained by Ms. Michelle, I talked to him even though he wasn't coherent. I said a small prayer for his comfort and his family. His lips started turning blue at the end of my shift, around 1400 hours, and he was pronounced dead by the end of the night.

Nursing For The Few

Nursing for some is a natural progression, an extension of a way of life. A person doesn't just decide one day to be caring and compassionate, they simply are by nature. Choosing a career caring for the sick and dying is a big decision and to be taken seriously. Nursing is a desirable career choice for making a reasonable living, plus it is not one of the disappearing jobs of the future. Regrettably, nursing has become popular primarily for being a relatively good pay check. If someone is looking for a stable career, nursing seems to be an easy answer. However, if money is the only object then the dark side of nursing is that it draws the wrong type of individual. For example, from my experience, one does not need to be a particularly savoury character to be successful in software engineering.

Being a nurse doesn't carry the same burden as being a physician. Becoming a doctor is a serious decision and is more than just a job. A doctor doesn't stop thinking like a doctor after s/he leaves the office or hospital. Of course, after leaving work or the end of a shift, health professionals can breathe a sigh of relief and unwind but they aren't changing who they are. They don't, we assume, transition from caring about people in their day job to abusing their friends and family once they remove their stethoscope.

Is nursing for everyone and anyone? Do people generally feel nurses are special people? Are nurses meant to be caring and compassionate in all things? Of course, they are human like all of us but the idea of a nurse being morally wholesome caregivers, more akin to Florence Nightingale or even Mother Teresa, is universal.

The history of nursing dates back 200-300 A.D., or the end of the Roman Empire, wherein people called 'nurses' worked alongside doctors. This is also the time when hospitals were established. Progressing into the middle ages, it was typically nuns and monks caring for the sick. In modern nursing times, Florence Nightingale was one of several prominent nurses; she cared for soldiers on the battlefield ("The History of Nursing." *Nursing School Hub*, 2021, https://www.nursingschoolhub.com/history-nursing.).

Her biggest achievement came during the wartimes when she insisted England send her sterile instruments and dressings. She changed the procedures of battlefield medical intervention by insisting upon better hygiene and sanitation. What followed was a decrease in soldier deaths from infection ("The History of Nursing." *Nursing School Hub*, 2021, https://www.nursingschoolhub.com/history-nursing.).

Scabies

It was a night shift and I was assigned to work in the 'short stay' section of the emergency department. This area is more closely aligned with a minimalist ward configuration. We call it a "step-down" from emergency care as these patients are stabilised and need a few more treatments of lesser urgency. For example, a second bag of intravenous saline or antibiotics; a final blood test to confirm or deny a diagnosis before discharge; several hours of rest following their emergency department treatment; several changes of dressings to a wound; monitoring behaviours post a mental health crisis; and "holding pattern" or waiting for a bed to free-up in a ward.

Scabies found on patients is usually indicative of poor hygiene. Scabies will appear after several days or even months on the skin as a rash. If we are not informed that the patient is coming into the department with scabies we wouldn't know it, you cannot see them. Although scabies usually provides a rash, sometimes the rash is hidden under clothing or in skin folds. Scabies is prolific, microscopic mites living on your skin and burrowing-in to lay eggs.

Most of the beds in short-stay are segregated with curtains that provide some visual privacy but zero auditory privacy. I was just starting my rounds on this evening's shift with the first patient on the list, Mr. Arthur. He was in ED for a catheter change. He happened to be in the only room with a door. This room is often an isolation room for patients with the flu or other transmissible diseases. Inside the room was a bed, chair, table, intravenous mobile support pole ("IV trolley"), and all the oxygen, masks, emergency supplies as commonly found in every room.

While I'm focused on patient-centered care, of course, I also engage with the person or persons accompanying the patient. Seated in the corner of this room was an older, bedraggled man, messy hair, scruffy beard, stained shirt and jeans, muddy shoes. I introduced myself and he revealed to me, upon my questioning, that he was the carer. The patient was similarly disheveled, smelled of urine and body odour. He was cringing and moaning in pain. It was a very disheartening scene.

The lights were low, the room was ice cold, Mr. Arthur was sitting up in the bed with a dark urine-stained catheter and bag attached to his leg. I explained that I was his nurse and would be changing his "permanent" catheter. It wasn't really a permanent catheter, it was a catheter that would be regularly changed for his permanent condition; his inability to control his bladder. The question was, why he didn't have a supra-pubic catheter? A supra-pubic catheter is a catheter placed into a surgically created channel between the bladder and the area of skin between the belly button and pubic bone. It functions easier, it's a more secure option to drain urine from the bladder particularly in those with obstruction in normal urinary flow.

Mr. Arthur was a kind, sweet older man, early 80s but looked about 95-years-old. I asked him if he preferred his carer to stay in the room or leave? He said he was fine with the carer staying. I set up my sterile environment, gloves, catheter kit, and cleaning supplies on a rolling tray at the foot of the bed. I was also gowned up with two sets of gloves. Mr. Arthur was disrobed and in a hospital gown.

I lifted his gown below the waist and did a short exam of his perineal, scrotum area. His penis was nearly white, coated in a flakey pasty matter, odorous, purulent fluid (pus) coming from the tip of his penis (or meatus). The perineal skin surrounding his penis was red with a rash and little sores. I was sufficiently shocked by this as most of my fellow nurses and doctors would be.

I was commenting out loud to the patient and the carer, who was more interested in the floor tiles, about the filth and poor hygiene of the catheter and surrounding skin. Without even a stir, the carer continued to look at the ominous designs on the floor nearest his shoes.

My mind filled with many questions. Distressed and disturbed, I began to interrogate this carer man. Who was he? Was he the son or nephew? Was he a neighbour or distant relative? Who did he work for, what agency? One thing of which I was certain, he was getting compensated for his handiwork, paid to look after poor Mr. Arthur. I advised him to clean Mr. Arthur's perineal area better or more often, to which he replied defensively, "I've told him to clean himself."

Upon completing the catheter insertion and education, I stepped out to speak with the doctor. He was sitting behind a long counter below which sat three computers spread apart. He was likely doing chart entries, updates, research, and other data requirements that we all do. I asked him if he wanted the tip of the catheter sent to the lab (on occasion we cut the tip off the old catheter and send it to the lab for testing various infections, bacteria); the doctor decided against it.

A couple of days later, I found a small rash on the inside of my left forearm. It was about four centimetres circumference with red blister-like bumps. This rash was very out of the ordinary and I went to my general practitioner (GP) for further examination. He brought out the big magnifier goggles and light. He told me, in no uncertain terms, I had scabies burrowing into my skin. I was shocked, of course. Where did I get this? I could not think of how I had been in close contact with someone with scabies. Certainly not my husband. Then I realised it was likely poor, filthy Mr. Arthur.

He represented to our emergency department about two weeks after I saw him. He was again admitted with a painful purulent penis, full bladder, and as it turns out a blocked, grotty catheter requiring a change. He was found to be riddled with scabies.

My impression and brief experience with Mr. Arthur was that of a quiet, soft-spoken, kind man. An old man in need of basic, deserving care. It is infuriating to nurses (and other hospital staff) when we encounter neglect of anyone. We see all of it as nurses and doctors: children, elderly, and mentally challenged abused and neglected. In our profession, we are patient advocates and because we will defend our patients, we are often met with anger, excuses, or hostility from the abusers. Elder abuse is quite prevalent in our society and an ongoing battle.

"Stanley" The Stoma

He had a bad case of shingles, poor Mr. Bob. He came to emergency from an aged care facility and I recall he was a positive, smiley guy. Mr. Bob required our help changing his blocked, non-functioning stoma. He was vomiting, bloated, and felt very uncomfortable.

I was his nurse and we spent some time chatting. From our conversations, he stated that he had very few family members living close by. This gave me pause, I imagine it is common for a family to leave an area, where their elderly family is settled, for work or other obligations.

My grandma, at 85-years-old and on her own initiative, moved into an independent living apartment at an aged care facility/community. She was a very healthy, vibrant woman with no illnesses or physical limitations. She settled-in comfortably, cultivated friendships and was actively involved as a volunteer managing their resale shop. She enjoyed herself and lived her life. Visiting her was pure joy; we had the best time together. I never heard her complain about living at this facility; "it" was never an issue.

"It" meaning the dreaded retirement community or aged care facility/community.

She actively and wisely moved to this apartment knowing she was ageing and wanted to ensure she would be, eventually, properly cared for instead of relying on family. I find this totally unselfish and admirable. However, everyone is different and some would argue against aged care communities. This is, absolutely, each person's right and decision.

    Mr. Bob and I spoke at length during his short visit to emergency. He spoke of his family, the care facility where he resided, activities he enjoyed, and his stoma he affectionately named "Stanley". I say 'affectionately' very loosely. I believe he found the stoma an adjunct, a sidekick, a prosthetic limb (if you will), a plastic gizmo add-on to his small stature. Something he had to manage; Stanley was in his care.

    I loved this story because for an old fellow, Mr. Bob took life, flying shrapnel and all, in his stride. He was unique in that he didn't complain; he wasn't a whiner. Just getting on with the rest of his life.

Frequent Fliers, Drug Alley, Full Moon

You start your emergency (ED) nursing career in the section of the department called drug alley where you care for the drug addicts, alcoholics, suicidal patients, and mental health patients. Then you move to the acute area where you have cardiac patients, bowel problems/obstructions, and kidney or gallbladder stones. Then after a couple of years, if you're any good, and you pass an oral exam, you go to the resuscitation/trauma ("resus") area of ED. This is, as you can imagine, car accidents, falls off heights/ladders/roofs, bicycle wrecks, falls off horses, stabbings, people hit by cars, all of it. This is the hardest part of ED. You never know what your shift will be like; it could be very stressful or relatively light, it's totally random.

After about two years in resus you get to move on to triage if you pass a resus exit exam followed by triage training and another exam. Triage area is at the front of the department entrance where nurses separate people into categories depending on their level of emergency. This area is where you are in charge of everyone coming through the door. You are deciding how urgent is their emergency and then placing the patient into an area of ED that is suited to their illness/emergency.

As nurses we see the devastation, people at their lowest when they're hurting, really sick. I think this level of despair gets to a person after a while. I rarely got off a shift and felt, "Wow, I saved that person", or "I helped change that life!" I get off my shift, run out the door to the safety of my car and drive home as quickly as possible. Nursing takes all you have. These large humans require full attention, lots of care, they zap every ounce of energy out of our little nurse bodies.

Ever hear about the full moon and a spike in emergency presentations? With the full moon, we get many unusual characters and incidents in the ED. It is a strange phenomenon the coincidence with a full moon and an increase in emergency services, including police and fire departments, they all get many more call-outs. Not sure why, maybe we're all werewolves in disguise?

In one night, for example, our busy little emergency department could have the following: results from burglaries gone bad; falling and cracking skulls; pedestrian accidents; stabbings; roll-overs in heavy duty trucks; cannabis 'overdoses' (patients vomit and have a compulsion to shower, Cannabinoid Hyperemesis); suicide attempts; domestic violence victims; drunks; old folks breaking bones; several snake bites; kidney stone infections; several heart-attacks (myocardial infarctions); and bowel obstructions. Very busy shifts, always a busy department. Hospitals are usually overloaded, over-capacity.

Working New Year's Eve is tough. There are many, many drunk, drugged, violent people that end up in ED. Often, instead of "sleeping it off at home", family or friends feel the individual is too sick to be at home. The individuals are incoherent, vomiting, unable to stand and are brought into ED for help. They are in a state of the usual indications of being severely intoxicated. The drunk or drugged end up being baby sat by nurses while the rest of the family leaves to go home. This means providing fresh sheets, towels, a bed, an RN to watch them as they vomit against the walls, bed, sheets, and nurses. Once they are feeling better after several hours we discharge them home. It is by far the biggest waste of resources possible for an emergency department.

"Drug Alley" is the name we gave the emergency department corridor of rooms where we usually place people presenting with drug overdoses, drinking excessive amounts of alcohol, and mental illness; a catch-all area that wasn't a trauma. I didn't mind working in this area except on holidays. The drunks and druggies presenting were outrageous. These people were on "benders" or were just getting sauced for the sake of a holiday and it was our responsibility to see they were safe. We provided a safe place for them to detox, dry out, vent, freak out, scream, hit, kick, spit, vomit onto our uniforms and across the walls.

We do our best to create a safe environment for all our patients. We care for all people that present to our emergency department regardless of their personal situation. We're here to help, albeit, we might moan and groan a bit.

Serious Errors

Every doctor and nurse has a story of woe, admittedly or not. A story whereby they made a bad call, a wrong diagnosis, a medication error, charted the wrong drug, or miscalculated the dose of medication. We're like anyone else, mistakes are human. For this reason, we have checks in place. However, there are times when the humans do checks but for whatever reason the checks aren't closely followed and errors happen. Similarly, pilots have checklists before take-off. There have been a few pre-flights when I skipped a step or two. The results weren't disastrous, thank goodness, but this is how accidents happen.

One afternoon, a fifty-year-old male, Mr. Dale, presented to emergency with alcohol poisoning. He described to several hospital staff that day, his background: going through a divorce; bottomed-out emotionally, physically; went on a 'bender' three to four days drinking himself into a state of delirium, and thus the presentation to emergency.

Soon after he was admitted, he developed diarrhoea. He then began vomiting and aspirated (inhaled his vomit into his lungs). Several hours later, once ED doctors declared him stable, he was sent to a ward. What follows is a sequence of unfortunate events that took place at the hospital.

Mr. Dale had lost much of the sodium in his cells with his severe dehydration (diarrhoea, vomiting, alcohol poisoning). Loss of sodium to this extent can affect brain cells, in addition to the whole body being terribly imbalanced of electrolytes.

Sadly, soon after arriving to the ward, a couple of nurses administering sodium IV fluids, miscalculated the dosage, administered the sodium too quickly and damaged some of his nerve cells. It's pretty complicated medically, but administering sodium into the blood too quickly (to over-correct severe low sodium or hyponatremia) can cause varying degrees of damage to the brain, sometimes placing the person into a coma.

As the first bag of IV sodium finished, Mr. Dale became unresponsive and a trauma team was dispatched to his room. Doctors performed an emergency tracheostomy, nasogastric feeding tube, humidified oxygen, and a catheter.

Now more alert but because of the tracheostomy he could not talk. From the aspiration earlier he developed pneumonia and was placed on IV antibiotics. He then went to ICU.

Just an incredibly unfortunate series of events for this man. We tried contacting his ex-wife but she could not be bothered. We were able to get his young son in to visit. Mr. Dale did recover but I am unsure for how long he will stay sober.

Nursing Informatics

My employer, for most of my nursing career, was a state-run, government public health system of hospitals. With my software engineering background, I recognised many areas where technology could improve workflow.

After a year working as a discharge planning clinical nurse, and unable to contain my enthusiasm, I found a technology need that would streamline workflow and provide a platform for gathering essential business metrics.

After I finished coding, testing, and installing the new digital workflow application, the twelve nurses in the department participated in the rollout over several weeks. The two main components were a digital patient report document and a metrics-oriented database. The objective was to move current patient reports (a core business component) from a paper-based format to a digital format to improve data capture quality and populate the metric database.

To thrive in today's digital climate, organisations must adopt new technology and prepare for rising digital trends. This proves more difficult in government where, traditionally, people lack change readiness. While individuals may have a desire to "work smarter" this does not necessarily mean embracing technology.

The rollout of new technology that I introduced and incorporated into this department of highly experienced nurses was exciting but demanding. The biggest challenge was adoption and motivating the nurses to change their routines and learn new computer skills. Two-thirds struggled with the change and as a result, some jeopardised the validity of the business metrics. The new digital workflow application was a success at reducing waste and redundancy, reducing costs, improving workflow processes, and collecting superior metrics. For example, what formerly took two administrative officers two to three days per week to process paper entries, the new workflow application completed in less than ten minutes.

Regrettably, there was an unexpected shortfall in end-user basic computer skills. A few end-users were resistant to using provided department laptops and tablets as they had "very small screens" and users were inexperienced using a mousepad. User frustration, lack of skill and will, and new routines ultimately were too ambitious and the team lost momentum.

The biggest challenge for the nurses was the change to their routine, learning new computer skills, and appreciating the importance of collecting data for analytics. "We are not computer people!" exclaimed one nurse.

What was discovered during rollout training was significant knowledge gaps for the majority of users, including: understanding file formats; directory structures/hierarchies; and how to use a laptop or tablet.

Regardless that the new workflow application used Microsoft applications such as Word, difficulties were attributed to users' lack of knowledge in saving and storing files to a shared drive, using a directory structure, and difficulties with the laptop and tablet screen sizes. This project should have focused more on end-user training strategies, something crucial before and during a rollout.

There's an adage: organisations do not change, people do. This makes sense when a culture is willing to adopt change. Discouragingly, this particular department lacked change readiness from the start. Initially, the rollout of the digital workflow application benefited from most of the nurses giving it a try. However, with very little training time, individuals' lack of willingness to continue practicing and working on their skills, poor rollout timing, and minimum management presence, ultimately the project came to a standstill.

Gastro

A more senior male nurse I was working with on one afternoon shift, had ten years emergency department experience at a big city hospital. On this afternoon, we worked adjacent to each other; he had a set of assigned beds next to mine. I was asked to give morphine to my patient, a 17-year-old with severe abdominal pain. As usual, we draw up and administer morphine together (always two nurses to check 'category 8' dangerous drugs).

The senior doctor wrote up 10 mg IV (intravenous) to give "stat" or immediately. This RN guy said, "Woe, that's a lot for a young person. Let's only give half and see how she goes." As a newer ED RN, I thought that was smart as the young woman had never had morphine before; she was 'opioid-naive'. As soon as the morphine began absorption into her system she had a raging headache and then vomited (a typical reaction for some to morphine). Doctors don't have all the answers - nurses sometimes do!

At this small rural hospital, several wards had a run of gastroenteritis or Norovirus (the nasty one that cruise ships get). With "gastro", a person finds themselves doubled-over for days with "V & D" (vomit and diarrhoea).

The ward infestation had originated from a person brought in from an aged care home who presented to emergency with symptoms of "runny stool" but we weren't sure what the diagnosis was until we tested and asked questions. Staff should have placed this person into an isolation room immediately upon arrival. Within thirty minutes this virus had spread like wildfire. Some of the nurses and doctors contracted it as it is airborne for a few days. Several hospital staff were out sick for a week and the hospital suffered from fewer staff.

Comfort

At times, we have hospital admissions called "social admits". This happens when a homeless person has nowhere to turn; a distraught or anxious person has no one to help; a family member of an admitted patient arrives that cannot cope at home alone. Hospitals are kind in this way, although it would seem that hospitals are also dumping grounds for whatever society cannot handle.

There have been studies about psychiatric or "mental" hospitals and institutions managing much of these patients but they have all closed particularly in the United States. EDs are very much a go-to when all else fails. This is one reason why emergency departments are inundated, overtaxed, always on full throttle, and the staff is exhausted much of the time. Regardless, we are always very generous and caring to all our patients as you never know what their story is at the time.

A 60-year-old lady whose son overdosed on heroin and subsequently died a week prior, came into our ED one evening. She was so distraught and beside herself, she called the ambulance; she did not want to be alone that night. As she slowly dressed into a hospital gown and I was getting her into the bed, she was a bit hysterical, crying, asking for valium, and explaining that she just wanted to be around people that cared.

Whilst she understood we weren't family, she told me she simply wanted to feel safe, comfortable and to "have people being nice" to her. She was a gentle soul and really beat down from her emotional roller-coaster that had been the past week. I brought her tea and biscuits, a warm blanket, and propped her up with a pillow. Regrettably, it was a very busy shift and I didn't have time to talk to her at length. She was content to just be with people, there were lights on, movement, much to distract her. We kept her overnight for observation. She saw the social worker the next morning to sort out some help.

Wood-Chipper Threesome/Mangled à Trois

In our emergency department, policy dictates that we're individually assigned a section of beds for the duration of our shift. However, some nurses enjoy working with a fellow nurse assigned to the adjacent section. They will share their patients' loads, helping each other with various duties. These duties may include: wiping-down the bed area and making the bed together; assisting with getting up to speed on timely medications; completing on-time observations (blood pressure, pulse, and temperature); and hanging IV bags. If your section of beds is getting slammed with heavy patients (lots of drugs, IV bags, bedpans/toileting, hourly observations) or quick turnover, that is, a constant throughput of patients, having that extra pair of hands helps. In the end, the extra help mostly benefits the patients.

    When working with some nurses they absolutely refuse to pair up or share the load. Effectively, the patients suffer because of the nurse's pride or stubbornness. Often nurses simply don't get along with other nurses on their shift or they don't find the others as skilled. This may cause them to not want to work with colleagues.

It was a busy shift, as usual, in emergency on this particular afternoon. I was working with a colleague, pair-nursing, whom I get along with and we work well together. I was working in "drug alley". We are usually alerted by phone or in-person about a patient assigned to our section; a heads-up courtesy.

Our team leader came up to me and told me that a woman and her entourage were on their way to my section. She warned me this woman was behaving oddly, crying, couldn't put a sentence together, but not necessarily on any recreational drugs. The triage level was Category 4, non-urgent (categories are 1 - 5 with 1 being immediate/urgent). This particular assignment was based primarily on the mental health triage tool, after clearing the physiological discriminators (alertness, breathing, pain, and bleeding). Per the triage nurse, this patient had visible moderate stress and anxiety but was cooperating.

Shortly after the team leader left, a middle aged woman, sandy blonde, short hair, average weight, and height, came into the area, walking slowly with her companions holding onto either side. They were followed by a paramedic. I looked at my colleague and we both shrugged our shoulders.

I received a handover from the ambulance paramedic about Ms. Faina. The handover is a verbal story from one clinician to another that usually includes details about the patient such as the following: medical history;

current complaint or condition; and physiological facts such as blood pressure, temperature, and pulse. The reason Ms. Faina called an ambulance was confusing; she wanted to see a doctor because she was "beside herself, in a panic, distraught about her friend in a wood-chipper."

Initially, I couldn't believe what I was hearing. I finished typing up the handover into the computer system, turned to the woman, asked if her guests could wait outside the room while I did my examination. About four people piled out of the room and one remained per her request. Ms. Faina blurted out, "This is my sister".

I began with the usual observations, including blood pressure, pulse, temperature, and an ECG (echocardiogram). I waited to take blood samples until the doctor arrived and requested them. Knowing that drawing blood initially upon presentation (for various tests) is standard procedure in emergency, this patient wasn't the normal presentation and may not require a blood test. This saves everyone time and, of course, needless pain.

Eventually, Ms. Faina was discharged after meeting with one of the mental health senior nurses who had consulted with her supervising doctor for the discharge. The staff was still scratching their heads as to why she was brought to emergency in the first place? She entered and exited our department with the same cloud of confusion; what was to be done?

Mental health consultants talked to her to calm her down but she didn't divulge much information about events leading up to her visit.

Therefore, she was discharged without blood or urine testing. There were no medications prescribed to her, no referrals or follow-up visits. She was advised to seek further mental health consultations and therapy in her own time in the community.

Per the newspaper, over the next few months, it was alleged two men had killed their friend, Mr. Craig, using a wood-chipper while working together trimming trees on Ms. Faina's property. Police had found Mr. Craig inside the wood-chipper on the rural property. All three men were, at various times, in an intimate relationship with Ms. Faina.

Apparently, Ms. Faina was motivated by money. She had increased Mr. Craig's life insurance policy and had his Will re-written in her favour. The threesome involved in Mr. Craig's murder were arrested and charged.

Skin Is An Organ

The integumentary system is a collection of cells forming your skin or outer protective layer. Tragically, many people don't realise this is an organ like any other and should be treated with the utmost care. Skin diseases are usually caused by bacteria, viruses, or fungi. Staphylococcus aureus (staph) infections are one example of more common skin disease. Then there are more serious diseases like skin cancer. Left untreated skin diseases can kill you.

There are many very nasty skin diseases often caused by untreated cuts or sores. Similar to the aforementioned diseases, your common garden variety of soil carries many bacteria (Tetanus, Legionellosis). Such bacteria can wreak havoc on not only your skin but if it reaches your bloodstream can cause life-threatening sepsis.

Being overweight can kill you in more ways than your usual diabetes, heart disease/cardiovascular disease, and stroke. Here's a story about an obese, 45-year-old lady, Ms. Adelina. She had a simple pimple under a large fat fold below her left hip (nearly down to the pubic area). She picked it. It is possible that her fingernail was dirty and further bacteria entered the sore.

Over a few days, the bacteria in her skin-break began growing and enjoying the warm, sweaty, festering, dark place. Not sure she was a very clean person as she may not have been cleaning under these folds. Before she knew it, she developed necrotising fasciitis (flesh-eating bacteria). It started slow and eventually ate a huge hole into her pubic area, and upper legs.

Ms. Adelina became septic (poisoning in the blood). She went to ICU then came out of ICU and was my patient on the neurology ward. I needed to clean the wound daily which was still a gaping hole. The wound was very painful and twice per day was cleaned and dressings were changed. She was on round-the-clock intravenous antibiotics and fluids.

Her gorgeous family would visit and stay with her for hours. They would laugh and reminisce. Her husband, in his 50s, now the only parent at home for their two teenage boys, often stayed overnight when he could. The boys brought in large printed photos of family, pets, home, and taped them to the white stark hospital walls. These images brought some life into her room to comfort her during her recovery. I really enjoyed her family. I found them to be caring and loving, close-knit and cheerful most of the time. They were helpful to the nurses, offering to carry a tray of food or move IV poles around the room to better fit the tight space.

Ms. Adelina's health prior to hospital admission, particularly her immune system, was not good. When she developed this infection followed by sepsis, her outcome was grim. As hard as we tried, we could not get on top of the infection. I was not her nurse towards the end of her time in hospital and was very sorry to learn that she died a couple of weeks later. I didn't have a chance to say goodbye to her or her family. I regret these times, when I'm unable to say a few words, to express a heartfelt apology. Regrettably, these situations happen all too often.

Death And Fluid

The neurology and stroke ward had a new patient, Mr. Brent. Circa 75 years in age, male, history of heart failure, unknown viral infection, and delirium, to name a few. On the day I was working, Mr. Brent had been on our ward for four days when he was changed from active care to palliative care. The poor man was close to death: not speaking or communicating and barely moved.

What was significant about Mr. Brent was the amount of fluid (the most I've ever seen) coming out of his mouth all day and night. It was greyish/brown and very foul-smelling; the same smell we always get with dying patients. We suctioned him, the fluids from his mouth, every 30 minutes into a disposable canister that held about two litres. We were, it seemed, constantly changing the canister. His eyes were opened occasionally and he was aware of movement and our presence as we rolled him, cleaned him, changed his clothes, linen, adult pads.

One morning a family member, his daughter, called and asked if the family from another state should bother flying into town? Would he die soon? I answered that call and told the daughter that he could die any day now. We don't know the exact time frame of Mr. Brent's passing, but the family should come.

As nurses, there are signs of pain that we look for when our patients are unable to communicate. For example: they will grimace; lash out with their hands, fists; moan or groan; an increased respiratory rate. He wasn't in pain, as determined by the staff looking after him, and since we weren't aggressive in the morphine doses, it was difficult to determine a reasonable time of death. He was on a very low dose of morphine as per the palliative care team for end-stage, dying patients. There are times when patients are in severe pain, given high levels of subcutaneous morphine (versus IV morphine), and we can more easily establish they will die within a couple of days.

Upon my return from lunch, I was told by the nurse assistant that Mr. Brent might be dead. When we entered the room, sitting in the corner of the room near a large window looking outside, drinking tea, and chatting quietly, were Mr. Brent's daughter and other family members. They were at a short distance from his bedside and hadn't noticed anything unusual or different about him.

Immediately upon entering the room and seeing Mr. Brent, I knew he was dead. He had stopped gurgling all that fluid in his throat. He was very quiet. The daughter looked at me and asked, "Has he turned a funny colour?" I gave the impression I was checking for his pulse and then turned to the family, stating, "I'm sorry he has died."

I stayed in the room to tidy up Mr. Brent's gown, sheets, and remove the intrusive devices attached to him, including the suction device resting under his pillow for quick access. The family gathered around the bed to hold his hand, to bow their heads and say a few quiet words. There was no wailing, crying, no one yelled out; it was peaceful and accepting.

I then told the team leader to call the doctor and let him know to do the official pronouncement of time of death. This is something which could happen up to six hours later, oddly enough. In other words, Mr. Brent could lay in the bed, very cold and dead for half a day prior to a doctor's visit. And this is what happened.

Paediatrics In Emergency

Not everyone likes working emergency "paeds" as the kids scream murder and the parents are freaked out. On my shift this particular day, working in the resuscitation area or "resus", we admitted a one-month-old neonate, Luna, with possible bronchiolitis. Luna was very sick and we called for a flight team to take her to the bigger city hospital. Within an hour we were joined by a NICU (neonatal intensive care unit) nurse and doctor from the big city hospital to help stabilise her for a flight to the city.

There were four of us trying to get her tachypnea (very rapid breathing) down to more normal infant levels and to get fluids into her little bloodstream. The problem was trying to insert a peripheral intravenous catheter (PIVC) – or cannulate her tiny, nearly invisible, veins.

Finally, one of our doctors was able to cannulate Luna, draw bloods, and start a bag of fluids. I was handed a very small sample of blood and was able to do two droplet tests (leukocytes, glucose, other electrolyte tests) on the spot with a device we have in emergency for quick results. This is in addition to sending bloods to the lab located downstairs.

We sent the two blood vials to the lab to verify our results and further tests to see if there were signs of infection (ie. increased white blood cells). Further, we wanted to test for bacteria, although this takes time as it needs to grow in a lab for several days.

Because inserting the cannula and getting bloods from Luna was extremely difficult, we were very careful with the small amount of blood we had collected. It was like gold. After only twenty minutes, I got a call from pathology. The pathology lab was kicking back the bloods saying one vial wasn't labeled properly (after I confirmed with two staff the label was good prior to sending). Both doctors were livid with the lab. I volunteered to go downstairs and in-person confirm the blood samples were from this neonate. Finally the lab accepted the samples and began testing.

After a total of ten hours in resus, it was decided that Luna was just stable enough to travel to a closer, bigger hospital (not the flight to the big city) for further stabilising before eventually going to the city hospital.

Bronchiolitis usually only affects younger children, many under the age of two. It occurs when there is swelling in the smallest airways in the lungs, called bronchioles, obstructing them and making it more difficult to breathe. It is serious for neonates, it can be life-threatening. This story had a good ending.

End-Stage Cancer

One very sick patient came into emergency, resus, for difficulty breathing in addition to a litany of diseases: end-stage cancer; chronic obstructive pulmonary disease (COPD); one left leg amputated at the knee (BKA) from diabetes; and one badly mangled right foot with no toes from diabetes.

He was just the nicest older man. Couldn't thank me enough for being kind and taking good care of him (adjusting bed positions, coffee, sandwiches, hot blankets, toileting, basic stuff). His cognition was good; he scored 15/15 based on the international assessment tool for neurological function, the Glascow Coma Scale (or GCS=15).

We chatted at length as he was my only patient in resus for most of the shift. He was an engineer, travelled the world doing consulting contracts on oil rigs, refineries. Initially, he revelled in his jobs in Iraq where he made several trips. He described, "At once profound and beautiful but also complex and torn."

One story he expounded upon was on the peninsula of Yemen, where he described many folks wanting to kill his small team. He knew in order to save their lives they had to flee the country. The oil company, his employer, hid them in trucks for a couple of days and eventually got them to a boat where they set off to a safer country.

A fascinating evening for me and I was so glad to have met this man and hear of his adventures.

Amputations Galore

So many patients are leaving hospitals with fewer body parts than when they arrive! I feel as though I work for a butcher shop. These patients do not appear to be very disturbed by this arrangement or they do well hiding their fear. While unfortunate to be leaving with fewer limbs, they are taking home with them some parting gifts: new prosthetics; mobility aids, and/or a new walking stick (cane) or four-wheel walker. Many of them are only 50 to 60-years-old.

At the start of my nursing education, we students were warned to never clip the toenails of our diabetic patients. And that was that, we weren't told why. Or it's possible, I didn't hear the lecture correctly and should have raised my hand to ask. Or perhaps, the educator thought we'd figure it out through telepathy or osmosis. Eventually, I figured it out on my own. The rule was applicable to our diabetic patients, in that, if we were to clip a toenail and cut it too low or cut the skin, the diabetic would not be alarmed as they might not feel the injury and an infection could set-in.

It may surprise you to learn that hospitals do many daily amputations; a multitude of toes and feet coming off. It's big business! Often it is gangrene that sets in and the extremity turns black. Not only is the extremity no longer of use, but in order for the infection to stop spreading, the limb and surrounding tissue also need to be removed. Sometimes extensive tissue are removed adjacent to the limb. For example, one of my patients had a black big toe. There was a small portion of the infection spreading into his foot. Before he knew it, his foot needed amputation.

Often it's the patient's fault. People don't take care of their feet. Particularly a diabetic person who has diabetic neuropathy or loss of feeling in one or more extremities (ie. toes). They really need to spend time with their lower limbs checking for anything out of the ordinary. If you have no sensation or feeling in your toes, you may stub your toe into a chair leg and not realise it. One day you see that a toe or toes have gone black! Now we have to amputate. We usually see lower limb amputations. Some are extreme as (AKA) above-knee amputations or (BKA) below the knee.

I know diabetes is very difficult to manage for many people. My intensions are not to cast aspersions on anyone. The disease is manageable with the right education and care. Sadly, at the hospital we see the results of mismanaged diabetes and devastating amputations.

Snake Bite

When she arrived, my first snake bite patient was a talkative, nervous, but stable, middle aged woman. She was feeling no pain. However, shortly after placing her in a hospital gown and taking her vital signs, she began to feel sharp pain rising from her left ankle (the bite location) to her thigh. I was already hastily inserting an IV to take bloods and start a "drip" or fluids.

She was bandaged up from her foot to just below her knee by the paramedics. I was told by the treating doctor we could safely remove her bandages and check the site. There appeared to be two fang marks or holes on her ankle, two bloody "dots".

Ms. Ann and her partner described in some detail a particular poisonous/venomous snake that, after striking her ankle, scurried away. However, when her partner stepped out, and when I questioned further, she couldn't say with certainty that it was the snake that struck her ankle, she didn't see this happen. She only knows she felt a sharp pain and then saw a snake slithering into the bushes.

Because several species of snake in the area can be venomous and therefore deadly, we take all apparent snake bites very seriously and begin life-saving procedures. She arrived by ambulance and I began recording a timeline of her injury and symptoms, starting with the time she believed she was bit up to the current time in emergency. This is a normal 'snake bite' procedure in emergency, including: stabilising the injured area; slowing the spread of venom; taking bloods at certain times; and taking vital signs frequently at certain intervals.

We are always skeptical but cautious of a patient's snake knowledge. As it turned out, this was not a venomous snake after our testing but the patient was fighting some infection in her blood regardless. When we told Ms. Ann of the good results, she was not convinced but understood it could have been her mistake.

When Ms. Ann first arrived, there were the bloody 'dots' that we both saw on her ankle. However, after about an hour or so, once the blood dried, I was wiping the ankle and the dried blood fell away. What was left behind was a woman's smooth, unadulterated, white ankle skin. In other words, it appeared as though I wiped off the two fang marks; no longer bite marks.

What was going on? Did she merely get hit by flying pebbles or gravel? Were the bloody dots or apparent holes merely blood spatter from something else hitting her ankle? It was very strange. I alerted the doctor and another nurse to my findings. We did not mention this to Ms. Ann, and after a few hours of observations, we let her get dressed and she was discharged.

Convict

Newly released from prison, living at home with his mother, Mr. Devin arrived in an ambulance, handcuffed, with a police escort. He appeared very sick, pale, dazed. He was placed into Bed 1 in the resus area. It was the start of my shift.

We worked out he was in a state of diabetic ketoacidosis (DKA), a new-onset. Basically, it is a shortage of insulin in the blood and the body tries to compensate by using fatty acids that results in acidic ketone bodies (increased acid in the blood). He didn't know he was diabetic. His blood results had dangerous levels of ketones at 5.5, glucose 20 mmol/L (high blood sugar), and 6.8 pH (low pH). DKA is a serious condition that can lead to diabetic coma or even death.

Prior to the police exiting emergency, Mr. Devin was placed under the supervision of hospital security for constant monitoring. We were happy to have security present throughout his stay. At this point, he was no longer cuffed by police handcuffs but placed into soft restraints used in hospital.

Once I inserted the IVC and started treatment, he became agitated very quickly. He kept insisting we let him go outside and smoke. When I told him that wasn't possible right now, he proceeded to chew through his IVC line and then went into chewing his restraints. Pulling against the restraints, yelling, spitting, cursing, throwing his head back and forth, the doctor quickly prescribed a sedative.

With four security holding him down, I took a needle to his buttocks. Many nurses shy away from this particular procedure: it is almost always with a violent patient; usually injected into their buttocks; one has to pull the pants down; the patient might see it is you doing the deed; and it can hurt. While it is a very unpleasant but necessary course of action, our security team realise the best manoeuvre is to turn the patient's head away from the nurse approaching with a needle in hand. The sedation does not take effect immediately, contrary to tv shows and movies, nor do we stab unruly patients in the neck with a needle.

Finally, after about 15 minutes, Mr. Devin relaxed, was calm. Many patients require more than one needle or a higher dose of sedative and wind up falling asleep after a short period. This is not necessarily a good thing as the drug is powerful and then we need to monitor their respiratory rate, oxygen levels, and other vital signs at close intervals. Sedation is potentially dangerous but necessary for the safety of staff and other patients.

Mr. Devin also had orbital cellulitis in one eye (inflammation and infection at the orbital/eye tissues) due to so many fights in prison. His eye was swollen, purple, and red, a sloppy mess of puss and blood. He also tried (just before his mom called the ambulance) to cut his odorous, infected, rotten tooth out of his mouth with a paring knife. We observed his mouth was swollen and bleeding. The doctors called the county dentist to book an appointment and have a look.

Endotracheal Intubating

Category one or "cat one" is for the worst of the worst, including: car accidents; stabbings; heavy bleeding; cardiac arrest; spine and head injuries; snake bites; difficulty breathing; and severe, uncontrolled pain. The start of my shift had been calm and cool but after an hour things began to heat up.

Simultaneously, we were hit with three cat-one traumas and our small unit was full. There was a snake bite, a motorcycle accident, and a young man having multiple seizures.

I was the team lead for the trauma unit nurses that night and along with the doctor had to triage the most urgent patients in our unit. This includes doing some initial checks, including airway, breathing, circulation, alertness, and responsiveness.

The snake bite was already stable due to the excellent work of the paramedics. The motorcycle accident victim was alert and chatty complaining of a painful shoulder. He was stabilised and on his way to x-ray with a possible fractured collar bone. The seizure guy was in a bad way: he was unresponsive to stimuli (even painful stimuli); his breathing was erratic; he was our number one priority.

As our multiple seizures patient was unable to maintain his airway (he could not breathe normally on his own), we had to quickly gather our allocated (pre-determined roles and duties for intubation) team for intubation: the ED floor team leader arrived to manage the documentation (or scribe); I was airway nurse (my first intubation, prior were dummies); and I assigned a circulation nurse for preparing and administering medications. This intubation was also a first for one of our resident physicians that night.

Rapid sequence intubation (RSI) is an invasive airway management technique whereby the doctor induces immediate muscular relaxation with a neuromuscular blocking agent. RSI is used in emergency departments, in field emergencies, or in ICU, and is the fastest means of controlling the emergency airway. I was glad it was a good trauma team, it went fairly smoothly.

Patients who are intubated are closely monitored 24/7 by a nurse. This is unlike TV shows and movies, where intubated patients are often shown all alone, isolated. Imagine a tube down your throat and into your lungs attached to a ventilator machine breathing for you. You are not awake as this would be incredibly uncomfortable and stressful, not to mention painful. As such, similar to ICU patients, there is always a nurse within eye contact. Intubating is very serious and a patient's breathing lifeline. Of course, you want someone trained in this procedure which includes the artificial lung ventilator devices.

Comprehensive ventilation courses are conducted for resus-area emergency nurses, including training in the following: PAO (airway opening pressure), PALv (alveoli pressure), gas diffusion, PaO2, CO2, O2, FiO2, time constant, airway resistance and compliance, PEEP, autoPEEP, gas flow, waveform, gas pH, preload, afterload, and dead space.

We had to intubate twice, regrettably, as the attending doctor thought the cuff/balloon (inflates to seal gaps in the trachea/throat area) on the tube that went down the throat was faulty with a hole (a very, very rare occurrence). When the resident pulled the tube out, per instructions from the attending doctor, we could see it was fully inflated. Ouch! It was decided that it was the resident doctor's adjustments to the intubation tube when trying to make room for placing the nasogastric tube - the intubation tube balloon lost its footing, so to speak, and therefore the seal was broken, not the balloon/cuff.

I'm just glad the patient wasn't conscious when the inflated balloon was removed. The main reason for the nasogastric tubing, along with intubating, is for collecting stomach acid contents in the event of reflux or vomiting. We don't want vomit to enter the trachea or the lungs while a patient is intubated.

Motorcycle

My first bike was a 250cc Ninja. I dropped it several times before I graduated to a bike with more power. The new bike, a fun 650cc SV Suzuki, had more 'presence' or was more visible on the road. Disastrously, I had a bad crash on that bike when my back tire slipped on a white stripe at an intersection (during down-shifting). I broke my left leg. But I was not deterred. I sold that bike and bought a 650cc BMW. I loved this bike. It was complete with heated grips and a power plug-in for a heated vest. We eventually sold it as we were moving country. I have not ridden since.

We often get patients from motorcycle accidents. We stabilise them and airlift or air-transport them to the big city trauma hospital. These poor people have big gashes to their heads, staples to secure them, many broken bones - bad wreck stuff. These are usually pretty hard for staff. Not all are dire, often we'll see minor road rash. But some are tragic.

In my early emergency department days, a young man on a motorcycle hit a car "t-bone" style and was brought into resus with obvious hip, pelvic, sacral area injuries. After x-rays, we would learn he had fractured several bones.

Fractures were in is hips, sacral area, femur, shoulder, and more. He kept blurting out in a quiet voice, saying, "I have to pee. I have to pee." Our team tried to help him by offering a "urine bottle" while lying in the bed, but he couldn't get the pee out. The ED consultant told the young intern, who was very obviously nervous with such a trauma, "Be calm, take it steady, identify your top concern, then next concern and go from there." The intern was very, very nervous. That intern went on to be a trauma rescue flight doctor.

    Our patient was stabilised and air-lifted to the big city hospital.

Guilt

A middle aged woman, Ms. Ruth, presented with seizure activity to our emergency department. Her seizures began after an acquired brain injury (ABI) from a stroke 20 years prior. I saw the brain scans along with the other staff when we were reviewing her charts, history. Over twenty-five percent of her brain was blackened - or dead brain tissue.

Ms. Ruth's family was in attendance and more than willing to discuss what has been happening with Ms. Ruth lately. When I spoke to the daughter, Ms. Clarice, she explained that her mother just wasn't the same person for several years now and that her personality had completely changed. The daughter stated that her mother was displaying much more anger and some violence towards her husband (Ms. Clarice's dad).

I then spoke to Mr. Ruth, via a phone call I made to him; he was very upset. As with most family and/or carers, they are exhausted both mentally and physically. This is understandable for carers as they dedicate their lives 24/7 to the complete care of another human being as if they had a new infant. Typically, these are people in their 60s or 70s. He explained to me over the phone, "I'm getting so tired of her."

He wanted to talk to me for a while and I listened. He really opened up and let go of some frustration. He described his situation and wanted help. I suggested that at this point in her deteriorated state and his obvious exhaustion, that he get her into aged care or at the very least have a nurse's aide at the home for several hours per day to lighten the load. In addition, I explained to him that, "No, to answer your question sir, you're not causing her seizures, that is a result of her stroke." He then asked to meet me, "You sound very kind and nice. I wish to meet you."

As nurses and doctors we are often asked out (dating), asked to visit a patient's home for follow-up personal care, flirted with, sexually propositioned, touched and/or spoken to inappropriately by patients or their family, and requested to be a personal nurse/doctor. We are, of course, unable to engage and it is unethical to get involved in any such behaviours with patients or family.

When this older gentleman wanted to meet me outside of work and talk more, I responded in kind that I could not do this. I could hear in his voice a very sad, tired, but caring man who was lonely and likely in need of another's company. I would imagine there are so many people like him out there.

Inter-Hospital Transfer

Early in my emergency department nursing career, I was asked to do an inter-hospital transfer (IHT). This was a big deal and a necessary step in progressing through the tiers of the department. When I was asked to escort my male patient in the ambulance from our small hospital to the bigger city hospital, I eagerly answered with a positive yes. I had the training and was well-prepared and ready for the challenge.

There is a lot of policy and procedure associated with IHTs. For example, we do the following: we consult with the potential accepting clinician at destination hospitals; consult with our team about the transfer details, including plans; prepare the patient and possibly a caregiver for the transfer; complete an IHT referral form and checklist.

My transfer patient was an older male, car accident victim with the following diagnosis: bilateral hip fractures, low blood pressure, and tachycardia. I did a handover to the receiving hospital's RN describing the patient's situation, their diagnosis. I helped the paramedic and ambulance driver load him into the back of the ambulance.

Sitting opposite the paramedic and adjacent to the patient on my right, I was very nervous and wasn't sure what to expect. Would it be a slow ride? Would we hit traffic and put on the sirens? Would the patient become unwell and I would have to do some life-saving procedures? Would we get a flat or have engine trouble?

We arrived at the bigger hospital in about twenty minutes. I did another handover to their resus team in emergency and turned around and caught a taxi back to my hospital. It was a good experience for my first transfer.

My second IHT was to monitor an elderly man with a blood transfusion. Prior to loading the patient into the ambulance, the paramedics were dismantling the gear/equipment he was hooked up to in resus, including: oxygen; IV fluids; ECG; vitals reader (BP, pulse); and the blood transfusion bag of packed red blood cells hanging from a pole.

The paramedic took down the bag of blood and set it alongside the patient in order to transfer the patient from the resus bed onto the ambulance gurney. I was preparing my transfer pack (a massive bag that includes respiratory and circulatory support system equipment, IV fluids, and medications), speaking to the resus doctor about the transfer, and finally speaking to the team leader regarding my taxi voucher for returning to the hospital after transfer. There were two paramedics, one chooses to drive, the other sits in the back with the RN.

Once inside the ambulance, I set up my patient putting his blood bag up onto a hook inside. As we were rolling out of emergency's ambulance bay, I noticed the IV line to the blood bag had a substantial, long air bubble. This air bubble was crawling towards the patient fairly quickly as the weight of the blood came trickling down the line. I had to get rid of this bubble before it reached the patient's arm.

Contrary to popular belief, small air bubbles in IV lines are not necessarily deadly. Larger bubbles are a concern but a very small bubble may not cause an air embolism that blocks a vein or artery's blood flow. I won't give air bubble measurement details in this book. Best to ask a doctor. There is always going to be edge cases and we clinicians take all precautions to remove air bubbles in IV lines.

I pinched-off or pinched together (there was no valve in the IV line at this section) the plastic IV line just past the bubble and held on to it to stop the bubble from flowing further. I then took a 10 mL syringe, filled it with blood from the patient's bag, and replaced the bubble with blood by inverting the line and pushing the air back up into the bag. This was all done with two hands, travelling on a bumpy construction, gutted, gravel freeway.

Within a minute of finishing my bubble procedure, a warning light came on inside the cab of the ambulance indicating that the power was low and the truck needed to power down soon. The power indicator light was for the back of the ambulance, where the patient cot is located and all of the power supplied to the life support systems, not the truck engine. "What does this mean?", I asked. It means if the ambulance doesn't get plugged in and charged up (the engine doesn't supply a massive ambulance with enough power, it needs its own source to manage all the life-saving equipment onboard), the interior equipment will shut down, we'll have to pull over and call for a backup ambulance to rescue us.

We arrived at the larger hospital without having lost power. However, the ambulance driver did plug in once we were parked in the ambulance bay. We unloaded our patient and wheeled him into the triage area for arriving ambulances. I gave a handover to the doctor and nurse once we were properly admitted and all documentation finalised. Unfortunately, there was some miscommunication between the small hospital, larger hospital, and the receiving doctor.

The emergency physician to physician call before we embarked on the transfer was muddled with confusion about this patient's ailments and if he needed an ICU bed. This sometimes happens, doctors want to off-load a patient to another facility or a receiving facility doesn't want to accept a patient that isn't necessarily sick enough. I'm exaggerating here a bit, however, a turf war can ensue between hospitals and admitting doctors. I explained, to this ED receiving doctor, that we had sourced an ICU bed for him with this hospital's ICU department head physician prior to transfer and that is where he would be going after checking in.

After a few phone calls to ICU, the ED doctor was satisfied and our patient went up to ICU. In ICU I gave a third patient handover and left the hospital to grab my cab back to our small hospital. It was a great experience!

Spousal Confusion

Mr. Brayden, a patient in the cognitive assessment unit with severe dementia was being prepared to return to his nursing home. In my capacity as a discharge planner, I was to help with discharge planning and handover to the nursing staff at his nursing home.

I never treated Mr. Brayden nor was his nurse for any period while he was in hospital. Therefore, to do a proper handover, I began perusing the patient's charts and getting an idea about him and his stay in hospital.

As a discharge planner, we sometimes only have 15 or 20 minutes to quickly prepare a handover for discharge and get the patient out of hospital and the bed ready for a new patient. We assemble and organise whatever resources are available at that time. This can be tricky because we might miss a detail or two.

Further information can be garnered from the nursing staff treating the patient and that is where I went next. I discussed the patient's hospital stay and current condition with his RN on the hospital ward. She explained that lately, all he talks about is returning to the nursing home to be with his wife, living together at the facility. I took down notes about Mr. Brayden and his wife for handover.

When I finally was able to speak to the nurse in charge at the aged care facility to receive the handover, she refuted stating, "Brayden's wife has been dead for ten years." Very embarrassed, I graciously acknowledged our mistake to the nursing home's nurse-in-charge and informed them Mr. Brayden would be arriving at lunchtime at their facility.

Returning to the RN on the ward, I advised her of this "grave" error, to which she was surprised. Not really a very big deal, but knowing our patients' next of kin or married status (widowed) is helpful. To her credit, the kind RN had listened to Mr. Brayden for weeks talking about his living wife. I'm not sure how this little detail was missed but it has taught me to be even more diligent with my due diligence.

Encephalopathy

He was homeless and ate some regular, garden variety snails. Young Brad, in his twenties, dark-skinned, tall and handsome, was my patient on the neurological and stroke ward for several weeks. Mr. Brad contracted encephalitis. A parasite from the snails he ate that rendered him severely brain-damaged.

When he arrived, we understood he was homeless at the time and ate some snails found near the beach. He was without any identification when he was brought to emergency and finding his personal details proved difficult. After a week of searching the area with police, hospital administration was able to find family members nearby: a girlfriend with his two children.

The ensuing weeks that he lay in the hospital bed were excruciating for both the staff and his family. He was aphasic (loss of language/communication) as a result of his severe brain damage and did not communicate with us at all. He simply stared ahead or looked up or down. He rarely looked you in the eye. He was also lethargic, didn't move much, and required full cares, including feeding, bathing, and toileting. He was so young, in his prime of life, it was heartbreaking to see him in this state. We met his girlfriend and two small children in his room one day. She was vague, in shock I assume, but explained that Brad had several girlfriends and she was no longer in a relationship with him. The children seemed very confused and uninterested.

He was under the care of a full team of specialists, including physical and speech therapists. We, nurses, tried to communicate with him as much as we could. We sang, chatted, asked him questions, showed him pictures, and played music. We were trying to stimulate his senses to get some response. Eventually, we realised it would take time, many years of therapy to help him regain some brain activity, if at all. He was sent to a nursing home and I've not heard of him since.

Lockdown Area for Violent Patients

#1

I required security three times to help the nurses and staff with a biting female patient and an angry big man. It became a bit scary at one point. We weren't going into the lockdown area until we had a security team with us. But it worked out in the end and is always interesting. The only lockdown or locked section of the hospital is in the neurology and stroke ward on the third floor or in the basement for mental health.

During my time as an RN working on this ward, the secured area had four bedrooms (including a bathroom in each room), two beds in each room, a very small nurses' station adjacent to the medication room (shared by the rest of the ward), and a bright general area or common area to look outside large windows. In this common area patients could mingle, watch TV, play board games, and eat meals. The large picture windows were more than just pretty to look out, they were heavy safety glass; a thick polycarbonate tempered laminated glazing.

Another use for this common area is for late night close monitoring of a patient's sleep if they are disruptive in their shared room. We would roll the patient in their bed out of their room to the large room to keep a closer eye.

This section of the ward had three entry points: the nurses station (a locked door); the main entrance, a double-door entry plus, just beyond the doors, a double-wide steel gate nearly as tall as the ceiling; and a third 'fire door' exit in the common area that was used by firefighters or other service personnel. The fire door exit went onto a landing with steps leading down the three flights.

The windows are important as they provide a more caring, home-like atmosphere with views of large trees, distractions to birds, pedestrians walking below, cars passing, and weather. The windows help with the overall well-being of both patients, families, and staff. Unsurprisingly to staff, the windows were attacked by patients in an attempt to break out or to break glass in a rage. Some patients were very strong and would lift big chairs or small tables and throw them at the windows.

We would not stay in the room very long once these activities started. We wore one emergency call device that included a waist-clamped phone/radio transceiver used during each shift complete with a pull string for critical 'no time to make a call' emergencies. There were always at least two staff in the locked section for safety, including an RN and an assistant nurse.

#2

Two very big men were in lockdown at the same time. One of the men was admitted because he took an ax to his son; the other a hammer to his mother. I just realised, on that day, we needed to be counting the forks and knives post mealtime, or use plastic. We mostly use real forks and knives in this unit during mealtime as we are all together in the common area feeding them and oftentimes there is family with them. Apparently, it's never been an issue or a question. I did, however, find a fork under a pillow several times.

Some of these patients aren't necessarily at the latter stages of dementia or severe brain damage causing them physical weakness. They are walking around causing trouble, yelling-out, spitting, biting, swinging arms and legs, kicking, throwing their faeces, walking around naked, refusing to shower for a week, throwing their food, refusing to eat or take medications, and picking fights with other patients and staff.

One woman patient was calling the men "dicks" and the women "bitches", non-stop, stirring up the patients into a frenzy. I told the ward doctors to get a good 'drug cocktail' prescribed for this woman who stirs up the group. She needed to calm down or all hell would break loose. The doctors did prescribe a substantial drug combination but then she was so drugged up (a functioning drugged-up mind you) that she was bordering on going catatonic. She began having tremors, slurred speech, dragging a foot, drooling, and/or going stiff as a board. A scary spot to be in for this poor woman.

Often the doctors are trying to titrate the drugs. They put together combinations of medications that will best suit the patient so they can go into more permanent care (or return to their nursing homes). These patients are only in hospital while their drug regimen is sorted and then they are returned from whence they came.

Bus Driver Stroke

A 58-year-old man, Mr. Ted, had a stroke while driving one of the city buses. He crashed the bus, of course, and it was big news here in our small town. He was my patient for a couple of weeks while in the neurology and stroke ward and he was an absolute joy to look after. In fact, he looked like my step-dad; I had a soft spot for him. Sadly, and with many strokes, he was aphasic (couldn't speak). He was in bad shape for a 'young' man but was strong and had a very good chance of full recovery. For his age, he was considered a young stroke survivor. Most of our stroke patients in the ward were mid-sixties and greater.

A few times during my shift, his fellow bus drivers, workmates, came to visit him. On one visit they brought some of his favourite music and a disk player. Mr. Ted had a huge smile. These guys really cared about their friend, it was apparent when they were gathered around his bed talking jovially and laughing out loud. I was overwhelmed by their kindness and thoughtfulness. Their visits were always pleasant. A nice change in a ward that is often full of sadness and despair.

Some patients, probably half of mine during my career, are just so gentle and easy to manage, to care for. They make your job not difficult or challenging but pleasant and gratifying. This is where I had my best moments nursing. While this might sound obvious, I really felt my best when nursing the patients that were kind and gentle. Still we can appreciate the struggle and challenge of caring for all patients, even difficult ones.

Cannot See

An 88-year-old male driving his truck with a caravan attached was pulled over by police for driving erratically. He admitted to police he was driving without his driving eyeglasses. The police revoked his driver's license on the spot and issued him with a warning to stop driving and get his eyeglasses sorted before driving again. He assured them he would and could call a relative to pick him up at the current location.

A couple of days later, Mr Bill (albeit uncomical, he reminded me of the story of Mr. Magoo), the very same man, is seen towing his caravan hitting poles, parked cars, and again getting pulled over by the police. They recognised him and brought him into emergency for an injury check, including cognition testing.

Mr. Bill was examined by the team and then he checked himself out against the doctor's orders after a couple of days in hospital only to return dehydrated and malnourished. I was his discharge planner, or rather his new care facility placement advisor.

He was initially pulled over by the police because he was swerving all over the road like a drunk driver. He was not drunk but couldn't see the road, signs, stops, or other cars. Although his license was subsequently revoked, he told nursing staff he had to keep driving as he was 800 miles from home and alone. So he kept driving, ended up pulled over again, and taken to our hospital. He needed my help getting his driving glasses. He needed some good food, fluids, and rest.

Mr. Bill's backstory includes a step-daughter in another state that was looking after him. She was only barely helpful in sending him a set of driving glasses to the hospital. Additionally, she didn't want him to return to her home. Apparently, this was his only family.

Often we have patients with very sad stories and complicated lives, especially the elderly. I felt so much for Mr. Bill. He was very sweet, gentle, and lost, really. All he had in this world was his caravan, his truck, and a pension. He was again released from hospital and we hope he is doing OK.

Charlie

I got up late. It was the weekend and I had the day off. I decided to cook a big breakfast. We lived on ten acres in a semi-tropical rainforest just outside of a small country town. The weeds, the plant growth, were getting out of control for us both working full-time. We had discussed buying goats, llamas, and then cows to stem the aggressive weed growth and thus forest fire danger. The house was at the centre, the bottom end of the property boundary, surrounded by semi-dense rainforest trees native to the area. Although a rainforest, it was very dry in the summer months. We settled on buying cows.

    I brought a big plate of eggs, bacon, potatoes, and toast outside to tempt my partner into coming inside to eat. I saw some commotion at the far end of the property. There stood my partner, two women, and two big cows. This was a surprise! But I was so excited, I left the plate of food on the outside bench and made my way over to the livestock.

    Feeding on the weeds were two Scottish galloway, short, stocky cows. One was black, one was tan, both boys, both adorable. They were ours.

    Over the next year, we moved our portable electric fencing around the ten acres to accommodate the cows and get them to feed on areas of the property as needed. We usually fenced-off half an acre at a time for a few days until the cows were bored and lowed loud for us to hear. We learned from the original owners that the cows really enjoyed an occasional snack. I brought them some oats, barley, and molasses mixed in a bucket. This was the treat of treats. Nothing was going to disturb their gnawing, crunching, pure enjoyment of sugary-covered muesli. This treat, offering them a good whiff, and they would follow me anywhere.

On several occasions, the bucket of sweets was helpful when they escaped underneath the electric fence (it wasn't very powerful) to the neighbours' paddock beyond our property, down the back dirt roads. Here I would find them chewing the cud, sun baking, and lounging by a brilliant blue lake on a pristine emerald lawn. It was a completely fabulous experience for them, living like kings, and very much unlike our rough and tumble rocky, weedy, thorny, tree saturated property. But all things must come to an end and with a big bucket of the magic dust, all the way home we walked together, little tastes along the way.

Charlie was the big boy, tan, muscular, very friendly. Romeo was his partner and he was young, small, a tough little cow always trying to butt heads with us or our other pets (cats). Regardless we loved them both. I spent much of my days off brushing and bathing them, removing ticks and leeches, feeding them fresh hay, and sitting with them. Romeo allowed me to indulge in some special care only when Charlie was next to him.

Out doing some fencing work, I noticed that Charlie had lost some weight. I didn't think much of it until a week later he really looked gaunt. It happened so fast. I knew something was terribly wrong with him. I planned to call our vet after the weekend. We had the boys for about six months and our country vet came the first week we adopted them to give them a good exam and a few vaccines. They were fine and healthy.

However, after the weekend, on Monday, there was no sign of Charlie. I could not find him anywhere on our ten acres. He had escaped the electric fence (easy to do) and was gone. Little Romeo was still inside the fencing. I was so worried and had no idea what happened to him? Was he stolen or did he run off to the heavenly paddock? I went and checked all the places he liked, nothing.

I had to leave for work and my partner said he would have a wander into another neighbours' property; a sprawling vacant 20 acres. He didn't find him after only searching for 30 minutes. We waited a few days hoping he'd return. Then the smell. I could smell death and knew it was him. I could not bring myself to find him and asked my partner to please try again. He found Charlie under the shade of a big tree, on his side, some bloating and very much dead.

I was crushed. Charlie was the sweetest guy, he had a huge heart, he was very affectionate. We had to call the county as registered cattle owners and they run tests to learn how he died; this was meant for the county's health and safety regulations. The results may show evidence of any diseases he was carrying that could impact other animals in the area.

Some animals will leave, wander off, from their pride, their gang, or pack, when they sense their death is near. Some say this is a myth but I know first hand it was very real for us. They do this both to distract any danger (predators sensing vulnerability or death) that may be nearby and allow the rest of the group to carry on. This is what Charlie did. He wandered off and died alone. Similarly, I find it heartbreaking to see some of my patients die alone. Although these patients are in hospital with staff all around, particularly in a ward bed, they may die alone in their room, quietly.

I've had my share of patients who have died in hospital without family or friends gathered at their bedside. There are several reasons for this, including: no family nearby and/or cannot travel; family don't care; friends are all dead (old age); patient dies suddenly in emergency; dying in a ward bed where they are terminal; a family member does not disclose to others that the patient is dying, has died.

This last entry about a family member blocking the rest of the family to visit and say last goodbyes (perhaps a power of attorney) happened to one of my patients, Ms. Sung. She was a busy professional, travelling extensively, and living abroad. In spite of this, she was dedicated to visiting family at every opportunity. She described her appalling story.

Too Much Power

Ms. Sung was aware her family was out having an enjoyable dinner with grandma. Although she could not attend, she heard all about the food, conversations, and laughter they shared. Three days later her grandma was dead. The following story as told by Ms. Sung:

Grandma was in good health, had her wits about her, and only took aspirin each day. She did not have any advanced illness, no terminal conditions was told by her doctor over and over through the years she was amazingly healthy.

Per my sister, nephew, cousins, aunts, uncles, and friends of the family, grandma was her regular self, fully aware, functional, happy, talkative, and enjoying the dinner gathering that evening. The following morning, in her room at her aged care home, she told the nurse she had a stomach ache. Hospice were called to take over her care and she was immediately moved to the infirmary.

Hospice is for terminally ill patients, at the end of life, usually death is only hours or days away. The hospice doctor, as his job dictates, did no tests, no MRI, no CT, no bloods, no hospital. In other words, he didn't seem to be concerned. Instead, he prescribed a morphine drip, no oxygen (morphine depresses the respiratory system), and no fluids (via IV or by mouth).

Grandma was too doped up to talk to anyone on the phone (I called several times). I asked the nurse, "Why not run tests or give her a tablet pain killer, but not morphine, are you trying to kill her?!" The nurse only relayed what the doctor was saying, "She might have a gall stone and infection but we don't know, we're keeping her comfortable. She does have a strong heart, this may take a while!" Take a while? Did he just say "take a while" for her to die from dehydration and the side effects of morphine? Is that legal? The effects of morphine may include bradycardia (slow heart rate), low blood pressure, and shallow breathing.

The power of attorney (POA) was my mom and she gave the "go ahead" and let grandma die with hospice. She did nothing to save her. There was no convincing mom. I could not get to her in time, nor did I have any power to stop the morphine and get grandma to the hospital. Our mom made sure there was no family allowed to visit, no funeral, no service, she was cremated immediately and the urn placed into the ground. This was clearly elder abuse and it had been going on for some time.

Mom took ninety percent of her possessions and sold them. I know this because I had a copy of her Will. Grandma's wishes, while alive and well, were documented and given to me. In her document she described wanting a funeral: absolutely not to be cremated; picked out her casket; wanted a full funeral service with flowers (even suggesting a cost for the flowers); wanted a write-up online or in the newspaper (gave me the costs of that); she told us the pastor she wanted for the service; the music; what Bible verses to read; and a poem she loved to be read. None of this transpired.

My grandma vaguely trusted her daughter, my mom, but was bullied by her in the last few years. It was not a fair and equal relationship; the POA abused her power over grandma. In addition, mom forged all grandmas legal documents to be in her name, removing all other names: Last Will & Testament, POA, Living Will, bank accounts, checks, CODs (certificates of deposit), and life insurance.

This was in addition to mom forging checks from grandma's bank account for several years (my sister and I saw the forged signatures when at the bank). The bank manager wanted to contact the FBI but grandma said, "No." I can understand why older people do not want "trouble" or to "stir up trouble" with families. This was her style.

We were tempted to take mom to court for all of this mess but knew it would not bring our grandma back to us. May she rest in peace.

Living Remote

Mr. Sam, a 68-year-old, living in the middle of a hundred acres, near no facilities, with his wife (a non-driver, non-native English speaker) and two sons with Down's Syndrome, breaks his leg. The couple lived on welfare as they were the carers for their two disabled sons.

This was a difficult case. Mr. Sam was the main contributor, support person to this family of four, including a ranch full of livestock, and he was rendered incapacitated. He couldn't do anything, including drive, work, shop, or care for the family while he was recovering in rehab. He asked the hospital discharge planner, me, to help with social services. He needed someone, like himself, to care for the family and ranch. He requested someone to drive to and from the store for groceries and other consumables. He asked for help with his leg, including: mobilising, showers, toileting, dressing; rehabilitation services at home; cooking help and assisting his wife with the washing/laundry/house cleaning; and he had cattle, livestock that needed tending.

There are plenty of ranchers in this huge state living on hundreds, if not thousands of acres, in distant areas, that could be in his shoes. This was, without a doubt, one of my most challenging cases.

Researching agencies close to or within range of his ranch, there were none. We were going to have to pay extra, get creative, and beg. Care agencies do not usually go beyond their defined areas of care, for anyone, for many reasons. Some logistical reasons include: the remoteness of the job; the safety of the staff member/s; transportation dilemmas; road safety; timeframe constraints; and length of contract.

I called several agencies, including: nursing care; domestic assistance; physical therapists; delivery services; a ranch hand(?). I was unable to find a ranch hand to assist with the cattle and other livestock. In addition, the social services that would be able to reach his distant homestead were busy, booked-up, and when they were available, could only offer two or three weeks of services. The government will provide two or three (extenuating circumstances, of which he was one) weeks of daily care fully paid. This was all very unimpressive to Mr. Sam who pleaded with me again on the severity of his plight.

I was unable to communicate directly with Mrs. Sam as she was a non-native speaker. Therefore, to assist her while she was on her own to communicate with various services, my next step was to find a translator within the confines of a tight budget. Mrs. Sam was without a driver's license and unable to obtain supplies for the family or ranch. Mr. Sam was not happy with my inability to supply a small salvation army to descend upon his domicile. Genuinely, he didn't have anyone he could call to help. Not too surprising, he had no other family in the state and he was a bit of a hot-head.

Before discharge, my team was able to organise, with extra funding, facilitating most of his needs, less the ranch help. I organised three full days of meals, frozen, to take home with him to feed his family (from the hospital kitchen). I left him with one task of organising help with his ranch. As hard as I tried, and with plenty of guidance and assistance from support services, this was out of our scope of practice.

This ordeal, initially, left me defeated. A truly unfortunate and difficult predicament, I could not fully satisfy Mr. Sam's nor his family's dire needs. I found myself digging deep to resolve underlying feelings of inadequacy, incompetence, uselessness.

In the end, I learned how to renew faith in my abilities by simply realising we did all we could. We had much to offer this patient and his family. Lessons I learned and, perhaps, considerations we must make to survive the unexpected, include (particularly if you live remote): being prepared for natural disasters and medical emergencies as best as you are able; getting to know neighbours, other ranchers, town folks; have good communication techniques, supplies (including language translation if necessary); and have backup transportation.

Death at 36,000 Feet

On a flight one evening to an international destination, I was seated in the first row of the (aft) last section of this coach class cabin, next to one of the food-prep areas. At the back of my cabin, past the last few rows, were the toilets. About half-way through the flight, somewhere over the Pacific Ocean, an announcement came over the intercom system asking for a doctor to please make themselves known to a flight attendant. I did not offer nursing help. As it turned out, I had a massive headache and a couple of beers already in my system and thought, "No way I'm going to assist"; I was in no condition.

Looking to the back of the plane, down the aisle-way from my seat point of view, I could see a small group forming in the last couple rows. There was an older, perhaps 85-years-old, petite woman lying in the aisle on her back, her family surrounding her in the adjacent seats. In this section of the plane, the last 4-5 rows, passengers were now being asked to quietly move from their seats to forward sections of the plane and into new empty seats.

A doctor finally came forward to assist and several people were performing CPR and using an AED (automated external defibrillator).

With each shock, her limp body jolted off the floor. This went on for what seemed like an hour.

As happens, when the family is in-situ, doctors and nurses perform CPR/defibrillation procedures until the family is convinced (for the most part) and the doctor is satisfied that the patient has truly ceased heart function and cannot be revived.

After trying to save this little lady, the passenger volunteer doctor 'called it' and pronounced her dead, noting the time in the current time zone, somewhere over the ocean. The family was now closing-in on her body, softly crying, holding, hugging their loved ones. There was very little commotion.

It was late and dark outside, the blinds were down, inside cabin lights were dimmed for sleep. Most passengers were sleeping and unaware of what just happened. I was able to stay in my seat and after a short time went to use the lavatories at the back of the plane.

As I passed the last row of centre aisle seats, I saw wrapped up with airline-issued blankets a body and a make-shift tent to cover the woman's form. Once a living human, someone's mom, sister, or aunt, she was now a ghost.

To most passengers using the lavatories, this was probably just a person sleeping across several seats. I did notice a large water-soaked carpet stain in the aisle. I attribute this to the fluids leaving the body at the time of death.

In my 20s, I dated a volunteer firefighter serving an area in San Francisco's east bay. He explained to me one day what happens to the body at the time of death. I was really surprised to learn the human body excretes all bodily fluids, including: faeces, urine, and sometimes stomach or oesophagus fluids. Then I became a nurse and it all made sense.

It was now day-break and preparing to land was uneventful. We were reminded to have all our documentation for customs prepared, passengers were instructed to return to their original seats, all blinds up, all interior lights lit. After we landed, looking behind me, the last row of the airplane did not stir. As we gathered our luggage, the head of the customer service made an announcement, "Please remain onboard until the chief of police and state officials have boarded the plane." Presumably, a coroner representative would also board the plane. It is possible there needed to be confirmation that nothing sinister or criminal happened to this woman before all passengers could disembark.

I tried to reconcile myself to this unfortunate flight as perhaps my exposure to flying 'extensively' for a while. Over five years, I was travelling to international destinations at least three or four times per year.

And although these were all tiresome long hauls, it was an exciting time. Did all these flights increase my exposure to more unusual circumstances such as a death on a plane or even engine/airframe trouble? Asking friends who also travel extensively, none have experienced death on a flight.

Upon deplaning, I recognised one of the responders and caught up to her. We spoke about the incident. I asked her how she felt about getting involved as a nurse, a fellow passenger, and how she felt about the situation, the woman's death. She said the small team of people helping were the flight attendants, of course, and herself, a nurse and an ophthalmologist doctor. She said she was glad to help out and was thanked by the staff once she was no longer needed.

I have since never experienced death on a plane and hope to never again.

Reflections On Nursing

The day after I left my nursing career, I went for a walk with my partner in the nearby rainforest about 50 km from our house. It was an epic day, it was nearly perfect. For the duration of 90-minutes, we saw absolutely no humans on the trail. The forest teeming with life, a sea of rich, brilliant green ferns at waist height. Towering above us, tall Eucalyptus trees with knobby, dark brown trunks, some hollowed with decay.

The path winding, wet, dark chocolate mud, tree roots bulging through puddles of fresh rainwater, moss-covered rocks lined the edge. Lizards darting from the track with each vibration of pounding feet. The air was cool, moist, a light mist easily lingered. Birds harmonising their rich, mellifluous song; frogs croaking in gravelly delight; butterflies fluttering; the rain pattering gently on palm leaves, the sound of hiking boots splashing and crunching.

Ahead of me was my partner in a shockingly bright, incongruent with the surrounds, red raincoat. Under the canopy, we let our minds wander, drift, be still. What struck me most that morning was the tranquil calm of nature. Holding back tears of joy, I thought to myself, I might be having a mid-life crisis.

Why write this story? Why not a story about software engineering with a bit on nursing? At every job interview, I attended for a nursing position, I was asked by someone on the panel, "This is quite a transition isn't it? Going from software engineering to nursing? What caused you to change careers? What was the motivation?" I would answer with something similar to always having a desire to be a doctor or nurse. This wasn't the entire truth. I wasn't comfortable explaining that I was really in it for the trauma and gore.

I decided to write my story because I wanted to share this extraordinary experience. Unlike software engineering, nursing places you at the core of, what I would describe as, the human condition. George Orwell wrote about the essence of being human, stating that "[...] one is prepared in the end to be defeated and broken up by life". As nurses and doctors, we are certainly broken up by life. We're imperfect and complex like our patients; witness to all that is human, such as mortality, conflict, birth, suffering, loss, growth, addiction.

For a couple of years post my departure from the emergency department, ambulance sirens were a big trigger. I would cringe, worry, feeling incredibly tense by the sounds. Another trigger was during occasional walks along a beachside park about four kilometres from my house. I would go on this walk, mid-day, prior to night shifts, to try and relax and prepare. It was a place that for most conjured up joy and happiness: there were families having picnics; children running, shrieking with excitement; old folks carefully navigating the footpaths full of playful youths.

But instead of great pleasure, these walks, the area, turned into a pre-night-shift nightmare and trigger for stress and anxiety. I felt completely alone and distanced from these scenes of delight and relaxation. All of which could be simply me feeling sorry for myself or feeling serious anxiety. I wanted so much to be these people, seemingly having not a care in the world. This anxiety has now all disappeared after a few years away from my job and I thoroughly enjoy the experience of walking to this tranquil setting.

Suffice to say, I did not appreciate the last couple of years nursing and probably why I decided to leave the profession. Although only eight years of solid nursing (ten years including school and in-hospital-training), what I was experiencing was likely burn-out. I understood nursing was patient-centered and empathy towards people was a necessary skill. But my ability to continue emotional and cognitive empathy was at risk. If nursing is for caring, compassion, genuine love of the field and people's lives, then I missed the mark.

I went into nursing thinking, "I cannot wait to see blood and bones poking out." That was one of the attractions to nursing and I experienced some of that too once I moved into the upper levels of emergency nursing. But even then, the stress of some of the trauma was so intense I really struggled. I found that the doctors had all the interesting work. Then again, they had the ultimate stress of life and death decisions. Even if I picked the career under false pretences, I sure did learn an incredible amount.

Like most nurses, I was exhausted at the end of my shifts. I didn't want to work nearly full-time hours (full-time nursing employment in the public sector is very rarely offered) but had gotten myself into such a predicament. To segue into a new, better paying, better hours nursing position at the hospital, I had to work two jobs: the old job and a few hours secondment at the new job.

Perhaps it is maturity, getting older, that drives us to want a better work situation or environment? A couple of my nursing friends have recently come to understand the complexity of transitioning to a new area in nursing. They are embarking on this journey and find it taxing but, eventually, a better opportunity.

It was very telling that my move - to clinical nurse and discharge planner, away from the grind of emergency nursing, night shifts, and chaos - did not result in much improvement or satisfaction. Although in my new position there were no nights, no trauma, no bedpans, I still found the work too patient-intensive. I'm not alone. There are scientific journal articles that describe a lack of emotional empathy and bias developing over time towards patients by healthcare workers.

Reflecting on my career choices, obviously, my professions were vastly different. There were dissimilarities between the people and of course the jobs. It is difficult to compare the two. However, for me, in the software engineering profession, people largely kept their emotions to themselves and vented their frustrations in a civilised, non-gun-shooting, high-noon manner. I've worked with some excellent nurses and doctors all of whom were humble, caring, considerate, and professional at every occurrence. And like any profession, there are a few unpleasant humans we must work alongside.

I've learned plenty over the years about people, not unlike what I've learned about myself. The train wreck that was the start of my second career was far from anything I've experienced. Was it a good life lesson? Did I progress and develop my understanding of the world? Have I become a better person as a result? All very excellent questions I still grapple with. When asked if I could do a redo (the last ten years), would I do nursing? Yes, for the wealth of information, the medical know-how, and the beautiful nurse friendships I developed. But, no, I think my computer science skills used towards a new profession would have been a better choice.

I have the utmost respect for nurses and doctors. Their job is physically, mentally, and emotionally demanding. Ask any one of these professionals and most will tell you they love their job.

Afterword

Road To Nursing

During the early 1980s, my sister and I would go with mom on weekend drives up to nearby Palo Alto for shopping at what I considered a relatively exclusive shopping centre. We did this outing probably every month from the time I was 11-years-old. We would pass a building with a big rainbow-striped Apple logo on the side. I found the logo pretty cool. I knew about Apple; we had a Mac at home.

Exiting the freeway towards the shopping centre, we drove down the winding, picturesque Page Mill Road. I would read the business signs, including: Hewlett Packard, The Wall Street Journal, and Agilent. I wanted to work on Page Mill Road since first setting eyes on this amazing stretch of trees, lawns, and fancy big buildings with famous names.

I planned to start university as a pre-med major. I wanted to be a doctor but was told only a very smart person with a desire from the age of five could do medicine. I believed that advice from my father but still, I was going pre-med my first year at university. Unfortunately, my plans for university were pushed back when my parents divorced, announcing their finances negligible and split-up. It was messy and I was lucky to graduate high school.

A couple of years later, money saved and my father committing to some of the expenses, I entered university in Oregon. With funds limited, I had less than three years in which to complete a degree. I chose a subject that I considered one of the shortest routes to a bachelor's degree: English Literature. Interestingly enough, as a child, I never developed an interest in reading and only read to get my assignments done in school.

Why I thought this course would be a quick and easy finish for me was illogical. I didn't like reading books. Nevertheless, it was an opportunity to assuage my dislike of reading and enter a higher echelon of education. I found as a literature major that reading a lot of books, articles, and journals wasn't so bad. I did pretty well. This would prove beneficial in my future as a consummate student. I would go on to study further subjects and gain two more bachelor's degrees and a masters in software engineering.

After graduating with my literature degree and working unsatisfying odd jobs, I returned to university to pursue a computer science (CIS) degree. During this time, I worked as a computer lab manager in one of the university's departments. I thoroughly enjoyed this work, including teaching computer skills classes in the lab.

As a CIS student, I was told about a women's computer conference called Grace Hopper Celebration of Women in Computing. Of course, I'd never heard of her before becoming part of the department's Women in Computer Science club. So off I went, flew down to San Jose, California, attending the three-day conference. One comment that has stuck with me all this time was from the keynote speaker, Anita Borg, who said something akin to, "You need to get yourselves to Silicon Valley and be a part of what is happening."

This was early in the dot-com phenomenon. The conference really inspired me and set into motion the next 15 years of my life. Besides being inspired, encouraged, and excited for the next step, I needed to move to Silicon Valley and get a job.

After the conference, I told my partner we need to get to San Jose and start our careers. I spent the next six months applying for entry-level programming or systems administrator jobs and landed one on Page Mill Road!

It was a start-up biotechnology, bioinformatics company retrieving and evaluating gene sequence-related information for use in agricultural and pharmaceutical products. The CEO was a wonderful lady, we got on famously. She was a notable pharmaceutical executive, scientist, and clever business woman. Her children would play with her Apple Mac laptop often at home and she would bring it back into work for me to fix. It was a pleasure working with her. Occasionally, she had small gatherings at her gorgeous home in a pretentious area in the San Francisco Bay. I was invited along with other scientist women from the small company. We drank and ate sitting around a crackling fire.

After almost a year working for this biotech, I was asked to join another start-up computer technology company. This was fortunate as six months later the biotech company was acquired by a large genomics group and closed our offices.

Fast-forward many years, I was growing restless and a bit blasé in computer programming. I considered working in other departments at my current job, regrettably, there were no openings in the areas that interested me.

Thereupon, after a successful career in software development, I wanted to find a 'retirement career' that would be completely different and see me working easily for another decade or more. I had plenty of options: I was willing to venture outside my field; willing to go back to school; financially stable; and had an opportunity to move to my partner's home country.

Having an interest in the medical field but unwilling to spend eight years earning a medical degree, I considered nursing. It would provide me with a comfortable, flexible schedule, some income, and a relaxed lifestyle. As it turns out, nursing would prove very challenging and why I thought it would be otherwise is purely ignorant.

Like so many, I enjoy a challenge and love an adventure; I found the prospect of nursing to be both. Embarking on this new career felt like the opening pages of a good story: exciting, new, mysterious, and unknown. I wanted to see and assist with traumas, see bones protruding from the body. But for me, working in a hospital seemed like a far-fetched prospect. The medical field was very foreign to me considering I grew up in a physically healthy family, rarely setting foot in a hospital.

Up until this point, I had approximately two hospital experiences, including: a high school year-12 senior final project where I volunteered in an emergency department; and for a broken leg.

Per the approval committee for our final high school year-12 senior projects, my 'Emergency Department (ED) Policies and Procedures' was a new endeavour and, therefore, required my formulating, creating, organising, scheduling, and outlining its goals. In addition, I set up meetings with the hospital administration for approval, explaining my plans that I will be permitted to meander and document the ED for two weeks. I planned to observe and engage with nurses, doctors, and patients in this rapidly changing, high-stress, vulnerable, and sometimes dangerous surroundings. All documentation was approved and I began my senior project at the local hospital.

On one late afternoon shift, I was about to leave as required (volunteers had strict set hours) when several victims of a multi-vehicle car accident arrived. I was getting my bag from a locker when a nurse asked me if I would please stay a bit later and help. I was very pleased to oblige and do whatever was needed. This was a small, regional hospital emergency department, maybe 15-20 beds total including a trauma bay. Several ambulances arrived, more than three, with patients having moderate to serious injuries.

One of the doctors working that night, a handsome man I recall distinctly, Dr. Marco, peered from behind a drawn curtain and asked me to come into the trauma bay and help him. I approached the curtain, drew it back enough to step in, and felt my stomach turn when I looked at the young woman on the bed. I held back my vomit. On impact, she slammed her face into the windshield, no seatbelt, she was not ejected from the car. Her left eye was nearly out of the socket, there was bloody flesh and hanging tissue, and everywhere on her face were lacerations. She was "lucky" it wasn't worse.

Dr. Marco asked me to gently, but firmly, hold the patient's arms down as he began to examine her facial injuries. This required me to lay across her chest with my face close to hers. She was alert and could see but it was a blur. I was holding her arms down, talking to her about where she was, who was in the room, the date, and the time.

With her voice loud and quivering, she called out, "What has happened? What's going on? What's on my face?" She was fighting my grip so she could touch her face. Marco reminded me to keep her hands away from her face. She had deep wounds near her eyes and I don't think he wanted her imagination to run wild with what she was touching. It would have been too much shock to learn her face was disfigured at this point.

Marco explained the procedure to the woman before commencing. As he inserted the first of several injections full of anaesthetic into her face around her eye, blood spurted high in the air like a fountain. The doctor had not given her much sedative and a couple of minutes into the procedure she began to fight me.

I was younger, 17-years-old, than our patient and a lightweight, so I climbed on top of her using my whole body to hold her down. Marco was a bit taken aback but didn't flinch and kept to his task. When he had finished and stepped out of the curtained bed area, I climbed down, and told her she was doing great, was in good hands and she was safe. Soon after I left her bedside, and the ED, I got into my car and pulled my seatbelt tight around my waist.

At the end of the two week project, I had thoroughly enjoyed the experience. The irony of receiving a non-passing grade for the year-12 project and then becoming an emergency department nurse, was not lost on me. The high school teacher coordinating and ultimately grading the senior year projects was not a big fan. I did not receive a pass "P" grade but an "F" for failure to meet expectations.

    Less about policy and procedure, the project became a study on empathy. As a consequence, I gained a better perspective and understanding of others' emotions, pain, fear, benevolence, and will to survive. I was not apologetic for the failing grade or the valuable experience, nor going in my direction in the end. What I gained was a pearl of wisdom I could carry with me and impart as I entered adulthood.

About the Author

JD Moore

Ms. Moore lives on the coast in a beach party town with her partner and two loud, disturbed cats. A former software engineer and registered nurse, Ms. Moore is now pleasantly retired and enjoying the serene but often wild outdoors - forever dedicated to a relaxing lifestyle.

When she isn't writing, she is caring for injured wildlife through volunteering at the SPCA wildlife rehabilitation facility, and running some painful yet lively half-marathons competitively around the state.

Upon finishing her masters in software engineering, JD's first career in programming was at various tech companies in Silicon Valley. While she enjoyed programming for nearly 20 years, she wanted to do something different as she edged towards midlife. JD decided on something completely foreign to her: a career in nursing. She received her nursing bachelor's degree and registration after moving to her husband's native country.

Her first book, A Stoma Named Stanley, was written from her nursing journal that she kept throughout her short nursing career. JD found so many of her patients' lives remarkable and fascinating and wanted to share their stories with others.

www.ingramcontent.com/pod-product-compliance
Lightning Source LLC
Chambersburg PA
CBHW072337300426
44109CB00042B/1665